The Updated

VERONA

Travel Guide

Complete Vacation Companion to Explore this Top Tourist Destination in Italy, The History and Culture, With Budget Tips for an Exclusive Family City of Love Adventure

Davina Quest

Copyright © 2024 by Davina Quest

All rights reserved. No part of this publication may be reproduced, distributed, or transmitted in any form or by any means, including photocopying, recording, or other electronic or mechanical methods, without the prior written permission of the publisher, except in the case of brief quotations embodied in critical reviews and certain other noncommercial uses permitted by copyright law.

Acknowledgment and Disclaimer

Efforts of considerable magnitude have been dedicated to ensuring the accuracy and contemporaneity of the information contained within this travel guide, up to its publication date. Nevertheless, we acknowledge the inherent dynamism in certain details, such as contact information, operating hours, pricing, and travel particulars, which may be subject to change. We assume no liability for any inconvenience that may arise from the use of this guide or for the precision and suitability of information obtained from third-party sources.

Readers are strongly urged to independently verify the information presented in this guide and to corroborate specifics with the relevant establishments or authorities prior to finalizing travel plans. We emphasize the importance of remaining vigilant for any updates or alterations that may transpire subsequent to the publication of this guide.

The safety and satisfaction of our readers are of paramount importance to us, and we express our sincere appreciation for your understanding of the dynamic nature inherent in travel-related information. It is our hope that this guide enhances your journey and serves as an invaluable resource throughout your travels.

Table Of Contents

Why Verona Should Be Your Next Travel Destination............ 6

PART ONE. INTRODUCTION: WELCOME TO VERONA................ 10

    1. Getting to Know Verona................ 12

    2. Best Time to Visit........................20

    3. Random Facts About Verona...........23

    4. Common Tourist Complaints and Solutions 27

    5. Cost and Budgeting.......................31

    6. Tips for Planning Your Trip............34

    7. What Not To Do In Verona............. 36

PART TWO. TOP THINGS TO DO AND AMAZING PLACES TO VISIT................ 42

    1. Top Attractions..............................42

2. Cultural and Historical Sites..........................72

3. Outdoor Activities..86

4. Gardens and Parks... 97

5. Local Cuisine and Dining............................100

6. Events and Festivals.................................... 112

7. Day Trips from Verona............................... 116

8. Nightlife and Entertainment......................132

9. Markets and Shopping Souvenirs............... 135

10. Verona for Families................................... 139

11. Verona on a Budget...................................142

12. Romantic Things To Do In Verona............145

PART THREE: ESSENTIAL PRACTICAL TRAVEL INFORMATION......................... **148**

1. Visa and Entry Requirements..................... 148

2. Getting to Verona... 153

3. Booking Cheap Flights................................ 158

4. Getting Around Verona................................161

5. Top Rental Companies................................ 165

6. Best Areas to Stay, Accommodation............171

7. Comprehensive Packing Checklist..............180

8. Staying Safe and Healthy............................184

9. Finance and Money Saving Tips.................188

10. Useful Apps and Websites.........................192

11. A Guide to Sports Activities in Verona...... 195

12. Job Opportunities in Verona.....................198

13. Tour Operator Companies........................ 203

14. Etiquette and Customs.............................207

15. Suggested Itineraries................................211

16. Basic Italian Phrasebook.......................... 217

CONCLUSION... 220

Travel Journal...222

Travel Puzzle..226

Verona Itinerary Planner.............................230

5

Why Verona Should Be Your Next Travel Destination

1. *Romantic Atmosphere:* Verona is renowned as the city of love, thanks to Shakespeare's "Romeo and Juliet." The romantic ambiance, highlighted by Juliet's balcony, charming streets, and historic squares, makes it an ideal destination for couples and romantics.

2. *Timeless Architecture:* Explore well-preserved historical sites like the Arena di Verona, a Roman amphitheater, and the Basilica di San Zeno Maggiore. The city is a living museum of architecture, showcasing Roman, Medieval, and Renaissance structures.

3. *Cultural Heritage:* Verona boasts a rich cultural heritage, evident in its museums, art galleries, and theaters. From the Museo di Castelvecchio to the Roman Theater, the city offers a deep dive into its fascinating history and artistic legacy.

4. World-Class Opera: The Arena di Verona hosts a world-famous opera festival, attracting music enthusiasts from around the globe. Enjoying a performance under the stars in this ancient amphitheater is an unforgettable experience.

5. Picturesque Landscapes: Surrounded by hills and situated along the Adige River, Verona offers breathtaking landscapes. Enjoy scenic walks, cycling tours, or simply relax in the charming gardens and parks scattered throughout the city.

6. Culinary Delights: Veronese cuisine is a treat for food lovers. Indulge in traditional dishes like Risotto al Nero di Seppia (squid ink risotto) and Amarone wine. Explore local markets and eateries to savor the authentic flavors of Verona.

7. Festivals and Events: Experience the vibrant atmosphere of Verona during its various festivals and events. From the grand Opera Festival to the romantic

Verona in Love celebration, the city hosts events that showcase its lively spirit.

8. *Day Trips to Surrounding Gems:* Verona's strategic location allows for easy day trips to nearby attractions like Lake Garda, Venice, and Milan. Explore the diversity of Northern Italy, from serene lakes to bustling metropolises.

9. *Charming Streets and Squares:* Wander through Verona's picturesque streets and squares, such as Piazza delle Erbe and Piazza dei Signori. Each corner reveals a piece of the city's history and a charming atmosphere.

10. *Warm and Welcoming Locals:* Veronese people are known for their warmth and hospitality. Engage with the locals, immerse yourself in their traditions, and feel the genuine friendliness that adds an extra layer to your travel experience.

Travel Journal

PART ONE. INTRODUCTION: WELCOME TO VERONA

Welcome to Verona, a city that transcends time and captivates the hearts of all who wander its historic streets. As you embark on your journey through this enchanting destination, allow me to share a glimpse of the magic that awaits you.

My own love affair with Verona began years ago, sparked by a dog-eared copy of Shakespeare's timeless tragedy. Captivated by Juliet's balcony and Romeo's passionate declarations, I embarked on a pilgrimage, eager to touch the very stones that inspired Romeo's words.

But Verona surprised me. It wasn't just a stage for a fictional romance; it was a vibrant tapestry woven with threads of ancient grandeur, artistic treasures, and the warmth of Italian life. I wandered beneath the awe-inspiring arches of the Arena, its whispers of

Roman spectacles transporting me back centuries. I lost myself in the labyrinthine streets, each turn revealing a hidden gem: a fresco-adorned church, a bustling market overflowing with local delicacies, or a charming artisan workshop.

One balmy evening, I found myself sipping a glass of Valpolicella in Piazza delle Erbe, the city's heart thrumming with life. Laughter spilled from cafes, street performers captivated the crowd, and the scent of freshly baked bread mingled with the scent of blooming jasmine. It was a scene straight out of a Fellini film, a perfect snapshot of Italian joie de vivre.

Verona isn't just about grand sights and historical echoes; it's about the little moments that steal your heart. Sharing a plate of pasta with newfound friends, watching children chase pigeons in a sun-drenched square, or simply savoring a scoop of gelato as you stroll along the Adige River – these are the experiences that make Verona truly magical.

I invite you to join me on this journey. Step into the captivating world of Verona, where every corner whispers a story and every experience leaves a lasting impression. Let the romance of the city embrace you, and discover your own unforgettable chapter in this timeless tale. Dive deeper into the guide and let's explore together.

1. Getting to Know Verona

The History

Verona's story stretches back millennia, whispering tales of empires, battles, and artistic triumphs. While its exact origins remain shrouded in mystery, its ancient heart beats strong.

Roman Grandeur (89 BC - 5th Century AD):

Founded as a Roman colony, Verona flourished. The majestic Arena, Ponte Pietra bridge, and Porta Borsari gate stand as testaments to this era. Trade thrived, and poet Catullus called Verona home.

Medieval Transformation (5th Century AD - 1405): Barbarian invasions ushered in change. The city saw rule by Ostrogoths, Lombards, and Franks before blossoming under Scaligeri rulers. Castelvecchio, a fortified bridge and castle, was built, and Gothic architecture flourished.

Venetian Rule (1405 - 1797): Venice's reign brought peace and prosperity. Piazza delle Erbe became a lively market, Casa di Giulietta attracted pilgrims, and Teatro Romano was restored. Renaissance art thrived, leaving masterpieces like Sanmicheli's fortifications.

Habsburg and Unification (1797 - 1918): Austrian rule and later, unification with Italy, brought new chapters. The city became a hub for Risorgimento, the Italian unification movement. Verona's cultural scene continued to flourish with the likes of Filarmonico theatre and museums.

Modern Verona (1918 - Present): Verona rebuilt after WWII and embraced tourism. Today, it celebrates its rich past while offering vibrant festivals, renowned opera, and world-class wine.

Today, Verona stands as a living museum, inviting travelers to explore its ancient streets, marvel at its architectural wonders, and immerse themselves in the echoes of a history that has shaped this enchanting city over millennia.

The Culture

Verona, a city with a cultural tapestry woven through centuries, exudes a unique charm that reflects its diverse heritage. The cultural essence of Verona is a blend of historical influences, artistic endeavors, and a deep-rooted sense of community.

Historical Significance: Verona's cultural journey begins with its Roman roots, evident in landmarks like the Arena di Verona and the Roman Theater. The medieval era saw the rise of powerful families like the Scaligers, leaving an architectural legacy that dots the cityscape.

Art and Architecture: The city's architectural treasures, including the Basilica di San Zeno Maggiore, showcase a harmonious fusion of Romanesque and Gothic styles. Verona's cultural wealth extends to its museums, such as the Museo di Castelvecchio, housing a collection that spans from medieval to Renaissance art.

Performing Arts: Verona is synonymous with opera, hosting the world-renowned Arena di Verona Opera Festival in its ancient amphitheater. The city resonates with the melodies of classical music, making it a haven for music enthusiasts.

Culinary Traditions: Veronese cuisine is a celebration of local flavors, from the iconic Amarone wine to dishes like Risotto al Nero di Seppia (squid ink risotto). Exploring the local markets and trattorias unveils a gastronomic journey deeply rooted in tradition.

Festivals and Celebrations: Verona's calendar is marked by vibrant festivals and events. The city transforms during the Opera Festival, and Verona in Love captures the romantic spirit. These celebrations provide a glimpse into the lively and communal nature of Veronese culture.

Warm Hospitality: Perhaps the most integral part of Verona's culture is the warmth of its people. Locals welcome visitors with genuine hospitality, fostering a sense of connection that enhances the overall cultural experience.

The Location and Geography

Verona's location and geography have shaped its destiny for centuries. Here's a quick overview:

Nestled in the North: Situated in northeastern Italy, Verona lies at the foot of the Lessini Mountains, offering stunning natural beauty. The Adige River, flowing from the Alps, cuts through the city, providing a vital waterway and scenic backdrop.

Strategic Crossroads: Verona's position at the crossroads of major trade routes played a crucial role in its development. It served as a gateway between northern Europe and the Mediterranean, fostering cultural exchange and economic prosperity.

Fertile Plains and Rolling Hills: Beyond the city walls, the landscape transitions into fertile plains ideal for agriculture. Vineyards of the renowned Valpolicella wine region sprawl across the hills, offering breathtaking panoramas and world-class wines.

Urban Landscape: Verona's historical center, a UNESCO World Heritage Site, is compact and walkable. Cobbled streets wind through piazzas lined with architectural treasures, creating a charming and intimate atmosphere.

Natural Delights: While renowned for its historical sites, Verona also boasts green spaces. Giardino Giusti offers Renaissance gardens with breathtaking views, while Parco dell'Adige provides a haven for nature lovers with its walking and cycling paths.

Accessibility: Verona is easily accessible by train, plane, and car. The Verona Villafranca Airport connects it to major European cities, while the high-speed train network provides convenient links to other Italian destinations.

Geographical Impact: Verona's location has influenced its climate, culture, and even cuisine. The mountains offer protection from harsh winters, while the proximity to the sea brings mild summers. Local dishes often feature seasonal ingredients grown in the surrounding plains.

Exploring Beyond: The surrounding region offers diverse landscapes and cultural experiences. Lake Garda, with its scenic beauty and water sports, is a short drive away. Medieval towns like Mantua and Vicenza offer historical treasures, while the Dolomites provide a glimpse of Italy's breathtaking mountain ranges.

The Climate and Time Zone

Climate: Verona enjoys a temperate climate, characterized by warm summers and cool winters. Summer temperatures, from June to August, range from 18°C to 30°C (64°F to 86°F), making it an ideal time for outdoor exploration. Winters, from December to February, see temperatures averaging between 1°C to 7°C (34°F to 45°F). Spring and autumn offer mild weather, creating pleasant conditions for discovering Verona's historic sites.

Time Zone: Verona operates on Central European Time (CET), which is UTC+1. During Daylight Saving Time (DST), typically from the last Sunday in March to the last Sunday in October, Verona shifts to Central European Summer Time (CEST), UTC+2. Travelers are advised to adjust their schedules accordingly to make the most of their visit and activities in Verona.

2. Best Time to Visit

Choosing the perfect time to visit Verona involves considering various factors to ensure an optimal travel experience.

Weather: The ideal weather for exploring Verona is during late spring (April to June) and early autumn (September to October). During these months, temperatures are mild, ranging from 15°C to 25°C (59°F to 77°F), providing comfortable conditions for outdoor activities and sightseeing.

Crowds: To avoid the peak tourist season and large crowds, plan your visit during the shoulder seasons mentioned above. July and August tend to be busier, especially around major attractions like Juliet's House and the Arena di Verona. Exploring during the quieter months allows for a more intimate experience.

Budget: Traveling during the shoulder seasons not only reduces crowds but can also be more budget-friendly. Accommodation prices may be lower, and you might find better deals on flights and activities. Be sure to check for any festivals or events that could influence prices.

Moving Around and Activities: Verona is easily navigable on foot, but weather considerations come into play. Late spring and early autumn offer pleasant temperatures for walking tours and exploring the city's landmarks. However, if you prefer a quieter experience, weekdays during the off-peak season can provide a more relaxed atmosphere.

Festivals and Events: The summer months, particularly July and August, bring the renowned Arena di Verona Opera Festival. If you're a fan of opera, this is a must-visit time, but be prepared for larger crowds. Verona in Love, held in February around Valentine's

Day, adds a romantic touch to the city. Consider attending these events if they align with your interests.

In conclusion, the best time to visit Verona is during late spring and early autumn for pleasant weather, fewer crowds, and potential cost savings. Tailoring your visit to coincide with festivals or events can enhance your overall experience in this captivating Italian city.

3. Random Facts About Verona

1. *Shakespearean Influence*: While Juliet's House is a popular tourist attraction, it's worth noting that Juliet was a fictional character created by William Shakespeare in his play "Romeo and Juliet." The house itself dates back to the 13th century.

2. *Bridges of Verona*: Verona boasts numerous picturesque bridges, but the Ponte Pietra is particularly fascinating. Originally built in Roman times, it has been reconstructed multiple times due to historical events, including World War II.

3. *Ancient Amphitheater*: The Arena di Verona is not only one of the best-preserved Roman amphitheaters but is also still used today for various performances, including operas, making it a living testament to Verona's rich history.

4. Veronese Wine: Verona is situated in the heart of the Veneto wine region, known for producing the renowned Amarone wine. Wine enthusiasts can explore the Valpolicella wine route to sample the local varietals.

5. Romeo's Banishment: In "Romeo and Juliet," after being banished from Verona, Romeo seeks refuge in Mantua. The journey between Verona and Mantua is relatively short, and both cities are connected by a historic route.

6. Historic Libraries: Verona is home to several historic libraries, including the Biblioteca Civica, which houses a vast collection of manuscripts, incunabula, and ancient prints.

7. Verona's Scaliger Tombs: The Scaliger family, who ruled Verona during the medieval period, left behind impressive funerary monuments known as the Scaliger Tombs. These Gothic structures showcase intricate artistry.

8. *Giardino Giusti's Labyrinth*: Giardino Giusti, a Renaissance garden in Verona, features a hedge labyrinth that adds a touch of mystery and enchantment to the overall garden experience.

9. *Porta Borsari*: This ancient Roman gate, known as Porta Borsari, stands as a reminder of Verona's Roman past. It's one of the main entrances to the historic city center.

10. *Verona's Interactive Art*: The city surprises visitors with interactive art installations, like the Talking Statues project, where certain statues "speak" through QR codes, sharing stories and historical information with passersby.

11. *Love Notes on Ponte Pietra*: Legend has it that writing a love letter and attaching it to the bridge's padlock ensures eternal love. While the practice is discouraged for preservation reasons, the tradition lives on as a symbol of Verona's romantic spirit.

12. *Kissing under Juliet's Balcony*: Beyond the tourist frenzy, this iconic landmark holds a local tradition. Veronese couples steal a kiss beneath the balcony on the eve of San Valentino (Valentine's Day), believing it brings good luck and strengthens their love.

13. *Verona as a Foodie Destination*: Verona is increasingly recognized for its culinary scene, going beyond the classic "pastissada de caval." Look out for innovative interpretations of local dishes, farm-to-table restaurants, and exciting food festivals like "Settembre Gastronomico."

14. *Sustainable Tourism Initiatives*: Verona is committed to becoming a more sustainable tourist destination. Initiatives include promoting cycling and walking, encouraging eco-friendly accommodation options, and reducing plastic waste in its historic center.

4. Common Tourist Complaints and Solutions

While Verona captivates with its beauty and romance, some common gripes can arise for tourists. Here are a few of the most frequent challenges and potential solutions:

Crowds and Queues:
- **Complaint:** Popular attractions like the Arena and Juliet's Balcony can get overwhelmed, leading to long queues and frustration.
- **Solution:** Purchase skip-the-line tickets online or consider visiting during off-peak hours or seasons. Research alternative, less crowded historical sites like Castelvecchio Museum or Teatro Romano.

High Prices:
- **Complaint:** Tourist traps and restaurants may inflate prices, impacting travelers on a budget.

- **Solution:** Seek out local trattorias and bakeries away from the main squares. Explore street food markets for authentic and affordable options. Take advantage of "pranzo fisso" lunch menus offering fixed-price meals.

Pickpocketing:

- **Complaint:** Petty theft can occur in crowded areas, leaving tourists feeling vulnerable.
- **Solution:** Stay vigilant, keep valuables secure, and avoid carrying large sums of cash. Utilize money belts or secure pockets. Avoid displaying phones or cameras openly.

Limited English:

- **Complaint:** While English is becoming more common, communication barriers can arise in smaller shops or restaurants.
- **Solution:** Learn basic Italian phrases like "grazie" (thank you), "quanto costa?" (how much?), and "parla inglese?" (do you speak English?). Use translation apps

29

or phrasebooks when needed. Be patient and respectful of language differences.

Limited accessibility:

- **Complaint:** Some historical sites and streets may not be easily accessible for those with mobility limitations.
- **Solution:** Research beforehand and inquire about accessibility accommodations at specific attractions. Look for hotels with elevators and accessible facilities. Utilize alternative transportation options like taxis or boat tours.

Limited Parking Spaces:

- **Complaint:** Finding parking spaces in the city center can be difficult.
- **Solution:** Use public transportation or park in designated lots outside the city center. Many hotels offer parking facilities, so planning accommodation with parking options is advisable.

Lack of Information Signage:

- **Complaint:** Inadequate signage can make it challenging to navigate the city.
- **Solution:** Carry a map, use navigation apps, or join guided tours. Municipal authorities could enhance signage to guide tourists efficiently.

Cultural Misunderstandings:

- **Complaint:** Tourists may unintentionally offend locals due to cultural differences.
- **Solution:** Research local customs and etiquette. Engage respectfully with locals and be aware of cultural nuances.

Noise Levels in Central Areas:

- **Complaint:** Some central areas can be noisy, affecting the overall experience.
- **Solution:** Choose accommodations in quieter neighborhoods. Consider noise-canceling headphones or earplugs for a good night's sleep.

5. Cost and Budgeting

Verona's charm caters to various travel styles, and budgeting wisely lets you maximize your experience. Here's a breakdown for solo, family, and honeymoon trips:

Solo Backpacker (5 days):

- **Accommodation:** Hostels with dorm beds (30-50€/night) or budget-friendly B&Bs (60-80€/night).
- **Food:** Self-cater with groceries from markets (20€/day) or enjoy affordable trattorias with fixed menus (15-20€/meal).
- **Activities:** Free walking tours, museum discounts with Verona Card (25€), picnics in public gardens, public transportation pass (20€).
- **Estimated Cost:** 400-500€

Family Fun (5 days):

- **Accommodation:** Apartments with kitchens (80-120€/night) or family-friendly hotels (150-200€/night).
- **Food:** Cook some meals in the apartment, explore kid-friendly cafes and restaurants with lunch menus (20-30€/meal per adult, 10-15€/meal per child).
- **Activities:** Verona Card for discounted family attractions (35€ per adult, 25€ per child), boat tours on the Adige (20-30€/adult, 10-15€/child), family-friendly cooking classes (40-50€ per person).
- **Estimated Cost:** 1000-1500€ (depending on family size and desired activities)

Romantic Honeymoon (5 days):

- **Accommodation:** Boutique hotels with charming views (150-200€/night) or luxury hotels with spa amenities (250-300€/night).
- **Food:** Indulge in fine dining with local specialties and wine pairings (50-80€/meal per person), picnic basket with local delicacies for a romantic sunset by the river.

- **Activities:** Private Verona Opera performance under the stars (80-150€/ticket), cooking class for couples followed by a wine tasting (100-150€ per couple), hot air balloon ride over the city (200-300€ per person).
- **Estimated Cost:** 2000-3000€ (depending on desired luxury and activities)

Essential Tips

- These are estimates; adjust based on your spending habits and priorities.
- Consider travel during the off-season for lower prices.
- Look for free events and activities, especially during public holidays.
- Utilize Verona Card for discounted entry to multiple attractions.
- Cook some meals at your accommodation to save on dining costs.
- Explore local markets for affordable and authentic food options.
- Take advantage of free walking tours and public transportation.

6. Tips for Planning Your Trip

Before You Go:

- **Season it right:** Consider shoulder seasons (spring/fall) for pleasant weather and fewer crowds.
- **Accommodation alchemy:** Choose your base wisely. Historic center is vibrant but pricier, consider quieter outskirts for budget-friendly options.
- **Verona Card magic:** This pass unlocks major attractions (Arena, museums) and public transport, great for active sightseers.
- **Embrace the app:** Download "Verona Tourism" app for offline maps, schedules, and insider tips.
- **Learn a few phrases:** Basic Italian goes a long way (grazie, buongiorno, etc.). Locals appreciate the effort.

Once You're There:

- **Walk this way:** Verona is compact and pedestrian-friendly. Lace up your walking shoes and soak in the atmosphere.

- **Free your mind:** Many churches and historical sites offer free entry, allowing you to discover hidden gems.
- **Beyond the balcony:** While Juliet's Balcony is iconic, explore other romantic spots like Giardino Giusti with its secret grotto.
- **Market marvels:** Immerse yourself in the sights, smells, and tastes of local markets like Piazza delle Erbe for fresh produce and souvenirs.
- **Aperitivo hour:** Join the locals for the pre-dinner ritual of "aperitivo" – enjoy a drink with complimentary snacks in buzzing piazzas.
- **Opera under the stars:** Witness the magic of an opera performance at the awe-inspiring Arena, even if you're not a die-hard fan.
- **Wine not?:** Explore the Valpolicella wine region for tastings and breathtaking vineyard views. Don't miss the celebrated Amarone.
- **Hidden gems:** Seek out lesser-known treasures like Castelvecchio Museum, Ponte Pietra bridge, or Torre dei Lamberti for panoramic views.

7. What Not To Do In Verona

1. Don't Touch the Juliet Statue: The bronze statue of Juliet in the courtyard might seem inviting, but touching it can cause damage over time. Respect the site and take photos without physical interaction.

2. Avoid Feeding Pigeons in Piazza delle Erbe: While it may seem charming, feeding pigeons in the main square contributes to sanitation issues and disrupts the local ecosystem. Enjoy the historic ambiance without encouraging this practice.

3. Respect Religious Sites: Verona is home to numerous churches with rich histories. When visiting religious sites, avoid loud conversations, and dress modestly out of respect for the sacredness of these places.

4. Don't Litter: Verona's beauty lies in its well-preserved streets and historic architecture. Avoid littering to preserve the city's aesthetic and maintain its cleanliness.

5. Refrain from Climbing Historic Monuments:
Climbing on historic monuments or sitting on fragile structures can lead to damage. Admire the architecture from ground level to ensure the preservation of Verona's heritage.

6. Avoid Peak Tourist Hours: To fully appreciate Verona's landmarks, try to avoid visiting during peak tourist hours. Early mornings or late afternoons often provide a more serene experience.

7. Don't Disrupt Opera Performances: If attending an opera at the Arena di Verona, refrain from unnecessary movements during the performance. Late arrivals and early departures can disturb both performers and fellow audience members.

8. Respect Local Traditions: Verona cherishes its cultural traditions. Respect local customs, whether it's queuing politely or adhering to dining etiquette in restaurants.

9. Avoid Over-Tipping: Tipping culture in Italy is different from other countries. While a service charge may be included, leaving a small amount as a gesture of appreciation is customary.

10. Don't Bargain Aggressively: While bargaining is common in some cultures, it's not the norm in Verona. Respect local pricing, especially in shops and markets, to maintain a positive atmosphere.

11. Overlooking the Hidden Gems:

- **Juliet's Balcony:** While iconic, it can be crowded and overpriced. Seek out romantic alternatives like the panoramic Giardino Giusti or the intimate courtyard of Casa di Giulietta.

- **Arena:** Don't just snap a picture and move on. Explore the underground maze used in Roman times, or attend a breathtaking opera under the stars.
- **Piazza delle Erbe:** While bustling, explore beyond the tourist stalls. Uncover hidden gems like the Torre dei Lamberti for unparalleled views or the tranquil Piazza dei Signori.

12. *Falling Prey to Tourist Traps:*

- **Expensive "authentic" restaurants:** Steer clear of overpriced menus with English translations in main squares. Venture into side streets for trattorias frequented by locals, offering genuine flavors at reasonable prices.
- **Gondola rides:** A romantic cliche in Venice, not Verona. Opt for a scenic boat tour on the Adige River, offering unique perspectives of the city and historical bridges.
- **Fake souvenirs:** Avoid mass-produced trinkets. Seek out local artisans selling handcrafted ceramics, leather goods, or regional wines and food products.

13. Missing Out on Local Experiences:

- Sticking to English menus: Ask for recommendations in Italian or use translation apps. You might discover hidden culinary gems.

- Skipping "aperitivo": This pre-dinner ritual is a social event, not just a drink. Join locals in cafes, enjoy complimentary snacks, and soak up the vibrant atmosphere.

- Rushing through: Slow down and savor the moment. Take time to wander, get lost in the labyrinthine streets, and strike up conversations with locals. You'll discover the true essence of Verona.

Verona is a city meant to be experienced, not just seen. By respecting local customs, avoiding tourist traps, and venturing beyond the beaten path, you'll unlock a truly authentic and unforgettable Veronese experience.

PART TWO. TOP THINGS TO DO AND AMAZING PLACES TO VISIT

As we delve into the heart of our Verona travel guide, Part Two invites you to embark on a journey through the city's most captivating destinations. From iconic landmarks to hidden gems, this section unveils a curated list of top things to do and places that promise to leave an indelible mark on your Verona experience. Whether you're drawn to the rich history, immersed in cultural gems, or seeking the perfect blend of romance and adventure, join us as we uncover the best that Verona has to offer. Let each chapter be your guide to discovering the enchanting tapestry of this Italian gem.

1. Top Attractions

1.1 Arena di Verona

The Arena di Verona, a majestic elliptical amphitheatre, reigns supreme as the city's crown jewel. Standing tall for nearly 2,000 years, it whispers tales of gladiatorial battles, theatrical performances, and grand operas under the starlit sky.

Situated in the heart of Verona, Piazza Brà, the Arena di Verona is conveniently located and easily accessible from the city center. Its imposing presence draws visitors from all corners of the globe.

History & Architecture:

- Built in 30 AD, the Arena boasts impressive Roman architecture with 72 arches and tiered limestone seating that once accommodated 30,000 spectators.
- Marvel at the intricate details like the "vomitoria" (passageways), Porta del Sole (monumental gate), and underground labyrinth used for stage machinery.

Visiting the Arena:

- **Opening Hours:** Varies depending on the season (generally 8:30 AM - 7 PM with extended hours during the Opera Festival). Check the official website for specific dates and times.
- **Tickets:** Purchase online or at the ticket office. Consider the Verona Card for discounted entry and other city attractions.
- **Guided Tours:** Explore the Arena's hidden depths and learn its fascinating history with a guided tour (available in several languages).
- **Accessibility:** The Arena is partially accessible for wheelchairs, with dedicated entrances and elevators.

Experiences to Remember:

- **Witness an Opera under the Stars:** The world-renowned Arena Opera Festival (June-September) transports you back in time with grand productions bathed in moonlight.

- **Climb to the Top:** Take the guided tour to the Arena's upper levels and soak in panoramic views of the city and surrounding hills.
- **Attend a Concert:** Throughout the year, the Arena hosts various concerts, ballets, and other events set against its stunning backdrop.

After Visiting the Arena:

- After your visit, explore the lively Piazza Bra surrounding the Arena, lined with cafes and shops.
- Stroll through the nearby archeological museum, Museo Lapidario Maffeiano, showcasing Roman artifacts found in the city.
- Discover the Porta Borsari, a monumental Roman gate near the Arena, once serving as a city entrance.

1.2 Juliet's House (Casa di Giulietta)

Juliet's House, or Casa di Giulietta, is an iconic destination in Verona that draws romantics and Shakespeare enthusiasts alike. Immersed in literary history, this 13th-century house is purportedly the residence of Juliet, the timeless character from William Shakespeare's "Romeo and Juliet."

Nestled in the heart of Verona's historic center, Via Cappello 23, Juliet's House is conveniently located near the bustling Piazza delle Erbe and other major landmarks.

- **The Famous Balcony:** The highlight of Juliet's House is, undoubtedly, the famous balcony where Juliet is said to have declared her love for Romeo. Visitors flock to catch a glimpse of this iconic feature, often leaving love notes on the walls and locks on the gates.

- **The Courtyard:** Upon entering the courtyard, you'll find a bronze statue of Juliet. Tradition holds that touching Juliet's right breast brings luck in love. The courtyard is adorned with love letters, inscriptions, and colorful notes left by visitors.

Visiting Tips:

● **Ticket Information:** Entrance to the courtyard is free, but there's a fee to enter the house and stand on the balcony. Consider purchasing tickets online to avoid queues.

● **Best Time to Visit:** Early mornings or late afternoons are ideal for a quieter experience, especially during peak tourist seasons.

● **Guided Tours:** Joining a guided tour can provide historical context and enrich your visit.

Practical Information:

● **Address:** Via Cappello, 23, 37121 Verona VR, Italy

● **Opening Hours:** Typically from 8:30 AM to 7:30 PM (may vary seasonally)

● **Admission Fee:** Varies based on age and type of ticket.

● **Juliet's Wall:** Adjacent to the entrance, the wall is covered in love notes, messages, and colorful graffiti expressing the enduring power of love. Visitors often bring padlocks adorned with initials, adding to the romantic ambiance.

- **Gift Shop:** Explore the gift shop for Juliet-themed souvenirs, including love-themed trinkets, postcards, and mementos to commemorate your visit.

- **Accessibility:** The courtyard and balcony area are accessible, but the historic nature of the building may pose challenges for those with mobility concerns.

Stepping into Juliet's House is like stepping into the pages of a timeless love story. Whether you're a literary enthusiast or simply seeking a touch of romance, this Veronese gem promises an enchanting experience in the midst of Shakespearean lore.

1.3 *Piazza delle Erbe*

Piazza delle Erbe, Verona's vibrant main square, pulses with history, charm, and local life. From bustling markets to frescoed facades, this iconic Piazza offers a sensory overload in the best way possible. L

History & Highlights:

• Originally a Roman forum, the Piazza has transformed into a lively hub over centuries. Admire the iconic Torre del Gardello clock tower, the frescoed Mazzanti Houses, and the ancient "Capitello" well.

• The daily market (except Sundays) is a feast for the senses. Browse fresh produce, local cheeses and cured meats, handcrafted souvenirs, and vibrant flowers.

Visiting the Piazza:

• **Location:** Right in the heart of Verona's historic center, easily accessible by foot or public transportation.

• **Opening Hours:** The Piazza is always open, with the market bustling weekdays from 8:30 AM - 7:30 PM.

• **Accessibility:** Cobblestone streets may pose challenges for wheelchairs and strollers.

Experiences to Savor:

• **Indulge in Local Delicacies:** Grab a slice of pizza, sip an espresso under the awnings, or savor gelato while people-watching in the lively atmosphere.

• **Hunt for Souvenirs:** Find unique handcrafted keepsakes, local wines and olive oils, and traditional linen goods at the market stalls.

• **Witness History Come Alive:** Visit the Casa di Mazzanti (House of Merchants) with its impressive frescoes depicting medieval life and commerce.

• **Climb the Torre del Gardello:** Enjoy panoramic views of the city and surrounding hills from the top of this 84-meter clock tower.

Essential Tips:

• Haggling is not expected at the market, but consider it a cultural exchange, not just a transaction.

• Be mindful of pickpockets in crowded areas, especially during peak season.

• Carry cash for smaller purchases at the market, though larger vendors may accept cards.

- Enjoy the street performers and musicians creating a unique ambiance.

After Visiting the Piazza:

- Explore the nearby Juliet's House and Casa di Giulietta, intertwined with Shakespeare's famous love story.
- Wander through the charming streets leading from the Piazza, discovering hidden gems and local shops.
- Visit the Museo Civico di Castelvecchio housed in a medieval castle, showcasing art treasures from different eras.

1.4 Castelvecchio

Cast your gaze upon Verona's imposing red brick masterpiece, Castelvecchio. Beyond its medieval facade lies a treasure trove of artistic wonders, housed within the city's renowned Castelvecchio Museum. Here's your guide to navigating this captivating historical and artistic landmark:

History & Highlights:

- Built in the 14th century as a military stronghold by the Scaligeri family, Castelvecchio's imposing architecture reflects its defensive purpose.
- Meticulously restored by architect Carlo Scarpa in the mid-20th century, the museum boasts modern design seamlessly integrated with the fortress's historical fabric.
- Explore diverse collections ranging from Roman sculptures and medieval weapons to Renaissance paintings and contemporary installations.

Visiting Castelvecchio:

- **Location:** Just outside Piazza delle Erbe, easily accessible by foot or public transportation.
- **Opening Hours:** Tuesday-Sunday, 10 AM - 6 PM (closed Mondays).
- **Tickets:** Purchase online or at the ticket office. Consider the Verona Card for discounted entry and other city attractions.
- **Accessibility:** The museum is partially accessible for wheelchairs, with dedicated entrances and elevators.

Unveiling Artistic Treasures:

- **Sculpture Galore:** Encounter Romanesque masterpieces like the Sepulchre of the Sts. Sergius and Bacchus, marvel at Gothic works like the "Crucifix" by the Master of Sant'Anastasia, and admire Renaissance sculptures like Cangrande della Scala's equestrian statue.
- **Painting Powerhouse:** Immerse yourself in Italian masterpieces by Mantegna, Bellini, Veronese, and Tintoretto, spanning religious themes, portraits, and mythological scenes.
- **Weapons & Wonders:** Explore the museum's impressive collection of medieval weapons, armor, and military artifacts, offering a glimpse into Verona's turbulent past.

Essential Tips:

- Download the museum app for an interactive exploration with maps, audio guides, and information about specific artworks.
- Join a guided tour (available in various languages) for deeper insights and historical context.

- Consider using the museum's cloakroom and free baggage storage if needed.
- Enjoy the museum cafe's light refreshments and stunning courtyard views.

After Visiting the Museum Walls:

- After your visit, stroll along the nearby Adige River or explore the Giardino Giusti park for its manicured gardens and breathtaking panoramic views.
- Discover the Ponte Pietra, a partially reconstructed Roman bridge offering historical charm and scenic photo opportunities.
- Treat yourself to a traditional Veronese meal at a restaurant near Piazza delle Erbe, savoring local flavors and soaking in the city's atmosphere.

1.5 Ponte Pietra

Standing tall over the Adige River, Ponte Pietra whispers tales of Roman ingenuity and resilience. More than just a bridge, it's a symbol of Verona's enduring spirit, partially reconstructed to stand once more as a testament to its past. Here's your guide to experiencing this iconic historical landmark:

History & Highlights:

• Built in 100 BC, Ponte Pietra served as a vital part of the Roman road network, connecting Verona to the eastern lands.

• Its five-arch structure and impressive stonework showcased Roman engineering prowess, standing strong for centuries.

• Destroyed during World War II, the bridge was painstakingly rebuilt using the original stones recovered from the riverbed, honoring its legacy.

Visiting Ponte Pietra:

• **Location**: On the eastern bank of the Adige River, easily accessible by foot or public transportation.

• **Accessibility:** The bridge is accessible to pedestrians and cyclists, with steps leading down to the riverbank.

- **Activities:** Enjoy a leisurely stroll across the bridge, soaking in the views of the river and historical surroundings.
- **Photo Opportunities:** Capture the bridge's majestic presence framed by the city skyline and lush greenery.
- **Relaxation:** Sit on the benches near the riverbank, listen to the water flow, and observe local life unfold.

After Visiting the Bridge:

- Explore the Giardino Giusti, a nearby park offering manicured gardens, hidden grottos, and panoramic views of the city and Ponte Pietra.
- Discover the Castelvecchio Museum housed in a medieval fortress, showcasing art treasures from various eras.
- Wander through the charming streets of the Veronetta district, uncovering hidden gems and experiencing local life.

Essential Tips:

- Consider walking across the bridge at sunset for stunning views of the river bathed in golden light.
- Be mindful of cyclists and pedestrians while crossing the bridge.
- Respect the historical significance of the bridge and refrain from climbing on its structures.

1.6 Porta Borsari

Standing tall and proud at the eastern edge of Verona's historic center, Porta Borsari embodies the city's rich Roman heritage. This monumental gate, once a crucial entry point, now serves as a silent guardian, whispering tales of emperors, trade, and resilience.

History & Highlights:

- Built in the 1st century AD, Porta Borsari served as a key gateway to the Roman city, controlling access and showcasing its power.

- Its impressive architectural details include two large arches adorned with intricate carvings, depicting deities, mythical creatures, and military symbols.
- The imposing gateway witnessed centuries of history, from Roman trade routes to medieval battles, forever etched in its weathered stones.

Visiting Porta Borsari:

- **Location:** At the eastern end of Corso Porta Borsari, easily accessible by foot or public transportation.
- **Accessibility:** The gateway is open to the public and freely accessible without entry fees.
- **Activities:** Admire the intricate carvings, imagine the bustling Roman trade passing through, and capture stunning photos against the backdrop of the city.
- **Interpretation:** Download historical information or engage with local guides to delve deeper into the gate's stories.

1.7 Basilica di San Zeno Maggiore

Verona's architectural landscape boasts hidden gems, and Basilica di San Zeno Maggiore ranks high among them. This Romanesque masterpiece, adorned with intricate carvings and steeped in history, awaits your exploration.

History & Highlights:

- Built between the 9th and 12th centuries, the Basilica showcases Romanesque architecture at its finest, featuring warm-colored stonework and intricate sculptural details.
- Marvel at the majestic bronze doors adorned with biblical scenes, considered masterpieces of Romanesque art.
- Explore the crypt, rumored to be the wedding venue of Shakespeare's Romeo and Juliet, adding a touch of literary intrigue.

Visiting the Basilica:

- **Location:** In the San Zeno neighborhood, easily accessible by foot or public transportation.

- **Opening Hours:** Monday-Friday, 10 AM - 5 PM; Saturday, 9:30 AM - 6 PM; Sundays and religious holidays, 1 PM - 5:30 PM.
- **Tickets:** Free entry to the church, with a small fee for the cloister and crypt. Consider the Verona Card for discounted entry and other city attractions.
- **Accessibility:** The church is partially accessible for wheelchairs, with limited access to the crypt and cloister.

Enriching Your Experience:

- **Join a guided tour:** Delve deeper into the basilica's history and artistic significance with a knowledgeable guide (tours available in various languages).
- **Attend a concert:** The basilica's acoustics create a magical setting for classical music concerts, especially during the "Settembre in Musica" festival.
- **Explore the cloister:** Discover the peaceful cloister garden, a quiet haven within the bustling city.

1.8 Scaliger Tombs

Verona's historic center holds numerous architectural gems, and the Scaliger Tombs stand out as unique and fascinating testaments to the city's past. These ornate mausoleums, perched atop arches over the churchyard of Santa Maria Antica, offer a glimpse into the power and artistry of the Scaliger family, who ruled Verona from the 13th to the 14th centuries.

History & Highlights:

- Built between the 13th and 14th centuries, the Scaliger Tombs served as elaborate memorials for prominent members of the Scaliger family, showcasing their wealth and power.
- Each tomb boasts a distinct architectural style, ranging from Gothic to Romanesque, reflecting the evolving artistic trends of the period.
- Intricate sculptures, colorful frescoes, and heraldic emblems adorn the tombs, depicting biblical scenes, historical events, and family symbols.

Visiting the Scaliger Tombs:

- **Location:** Adjacent to the Church of Santa Maria Antica, within the historic city center, easily accessible by foot or public transportation.
- **Opening Hours:** Tuesday-Sunday, 8:30 AM - 6:30 PM; closed Mondays.
- **Tickets:** Entrance fee applies, with discounts available for students and groups. Consider the Verona Card for discounted entry and other city attractions.
- **Accessibility:** The courtyards where the tombs are located are accessible, but the individual tombs are raised on arches and not easily accessible for people with mobility limitations.

Unveiling Architectural Wonders:

- **Scaliger Tomb I (Can Grande della Scala):** This ornate Gothic masterpiece, adorned with pink marble and equestrian statues, honors the most powerful Scaliger ruler.
- **Scaliger Tomb II (Mastino II della Scala):** This simpler, yet elegant structure showcases Romanesque

influences and features intricate sculptures depicting virtues and vices.

* **Scaliger Tomb III (Cansignorio della Scala):** This Gothic gem boasts vibrant frescoes depicting hunting scenes and allegorical figures, reflecting the ruler's love for nature and philosophy.

Enriching Your Experience:

* **Join a guided tour:** Learn about the history and symbolism of the tombs through a knowledgeable guide, available in various languages.
* **Combine your visit with other nearby attractions:** Explore the nearby Castelvecchio Museum, Ponte Pietra bridge, or Piazza delle Erbe for a comprehensive historical experience.
* **Admire the panoramic views:** Climb the Torre dei Lamberti (Lamberti Tower) for breathtaking views of the city, including the Scaliger Tombs from above.

1.9 Giardino Giusti

Step away from the bustling crowds and enter a tranquil oasis within Verona's walls. Giardino Giusti, a 16th-century Italian Renaissance garden, awaits you with its manicured lawns, hidden grottos, and breathtaking panoramic views.

History & Highlights:

- Designed in 1580 by Girolamo Giusti, the garden embodies Renaissance ideals of beauty, harmony, and perspective.
- Explore meticulously sculpted hedges, geometric flowerbeds, and trickling fountains, creating a sense of order and tranquility.
- Discover hidden wonders like the grotto adorned with statues and mosaics, offering a cool escape on a warm day.
- Capture panoramic views of the city and surrounding hills from the belvedere, a raised terrace adorned with statues.

Visiting Giardino Giusti:

- **Location:** In the San Zeno neighborhood, easily accessible by foot or public transportation.
- Opening Hours: Tuesday-Sunday, 9 AM - 7 PM; closed Mondays.
- **Tickets:** Entrance fee applies, with discounts available for students and groups. Consider the Verona Card for discounted entry and other city attractions.
- **Accessibility:** The main garden paths are generally accessible, but some areas with stairs or uneven terrain may pose challenges for people with mobility limitations.

Enhancing Your Experience:

- **Join a guided tour:** Learn about the garden's history, symbolism, and hidden details through a knowledgeable guide (tours available in various languages).
- **Attend a special event:** Check for seasonal events like concerts, theatrical performances, or art exhibitions held within the garden's enchanting setting.

- **Relax and reflect:** Find a quiet corner amongst the greenery, enjoy the soothing sounds of water, and savor the moment in this peaceful haven.

Giardino Giusti is more than just a garden; it's a living piece of art nestled within Verona's historical heart. By exploring its hidden corners, you'll experience the beauty and serenity of Renaissance design, capturing a glimpse into a bygone era.

1.10 Teatro Filarmonico

In the heart of Verona's historic center, a stage awaits. Teatro Filarmonico, an architectural jewel and cultural landmark, beckons opera lovers and theater enthusiasts with its rich history, intimate atmosphere, and world-renowned acoustics.

History & Highlights:

- Opened in 1755, Teatro Filarmonico is one of Italy's oldest opera houses, boasting a neoclassical facade and elegant interiors adorned with frescoes and stuccowork.

- Witness the stage where legendary composers like Verdi and Wagner premiered their masterpieces, adding to the theatre's prestigious legacy.
- Immerse yourself in the intimate atmosphere, offering unparalleled proximity to the performers, creating a truly captivating experience.

Visiting Teatro Filarmonico:

- **Location:** In Piazza Bra, right next to the iconic Arena di Verona, easily accessible by foot or public transportation.
- **Season & Performances:** Opera season runs from December to April, with various ballet, concert, and theatrical performances throughout the year. Check the official website for the latest program.
- **Tickets:** Purchase online or at the ticket office. Consider the Verona Card for discounted entry and other city attractions.
- **Accessibility:** The theatre offers limited wheelchair access and assisted listening devices. Contact the theatre in advance for specific needs.

Unveiling the Theatrical Experience:

- **Opera Under the Stars:** Attend a performance during the renowned Arena Opera Festival (June-September) and witness grand opera productions staged under the stars in the adjacent Arena.
- **Beyond Opera:** Discover a diverse program beyond opera, including orchestral concerts, ballets, plays, and contemporary performances.
- **Guided Tours:** Take a backstage tour (offered in various languages) for a glimpse into the theatre's history, hidden spaces, and technical workings.

Essential Tips:

- Dress elegantly (smart casual or formal) for opera and special performances, though more relaxed attire is acceptable for other events.
- Arrive early to avoid queues and soak in the pre-show atmosphere.
- Utilize the cloakroom and bar facilities if needed.
- Respect the performers and fellow audience members by maintaining silence during the performance.

1.11 Ponte Scaligero

Verona's skyline boasts many architectural gems, and the Ponte Scaligero, also known as the Castelvecchio Bridge, stands out as a majestic symbol of history and artistry. This fortified bridge, nestled alongside the Adige River, offers stunning views, unique experiences, and a glimpse into Verona's medieval past.

History & Highlights:

● Built in the 14th century by Cangrande II della Scala, the bridge served as a strategic military passage and a fortified entrance to Castelvecchio, the nearby castle.

● Its innovative design featuring three large segmental arches was considered groundbreaking at the time, showcasing the engineering prowess of the era.

● The bridge's walkway, flanked by crenellations and adorned with Scaliger family emblems, whispers tales of battles and power struggles, immersing you in Verona's medieval atmosphere.

Visiting Ponte Scaligero:

- **Location:** The bridge connects Castelvecchio with the city center, easily accessible by foot or public transportation.
- **Accessibility:** The bridge is open to the public and freely accessible on foot, offering breathtaking views from its walkway. However, the castle requires a separate ticket for entry.
- **Activities:** Stroll across the bridge and soak in the panoramic views of the river, the city skyline, and the surrounding hills.
- **Photo Opportunities:** Capture stunning pictures of the bridge from different angles, showcasing its architectural details and historical charm.
- **Combine your visit:** Explore the nearby Castelvecchio Museum housed within the castle, offering a treasure trove of art from various eras.

1.12 Via Mazzini

Verona's vibrant core boasts several captivating streets, and Via Mazzini reigns supreme as the city's premier shopping destination. This pedestrian-only haven, stretching between the iconic Piazza Bra and Piazza delle Erbe, offers a delectable mix of high-end fashion, local boutiques, and historical charm.

Fashion Paradise:

- Indulge in a shopping spree at renowned international brands like Armani, Gucci, Chanel, and Dolce & Gabbana, lining the street with their flagship stores.
- Discover unique finds at trendy Italian and local boutiques offering stylish apparel, handcrafted souvenirs, and locally-made accessories.
- Unearth hidden gems tucked away in side streets, showcasing artisan workshops and independent designers catering to diverse tastes.

Apart From Shopping:

- Immerse yourself in Verona's history at the Casa di Mazzanti, a 14th-century residence adorned with captivating frescoes depicting medieval life and commerce.

- Take a break at a charming cafe terrace, sipping an espresso or savoring gelato while people-watching and soaking in the lively atmosphere.
- Admire the street's architectural details, including ornate facades and historical landmarks like the Arco della Corte Real, a monumental archway.

Essential Tips:

- **Opening Hours:** Most stores operate from 9:00 AM to 7:00 PM, with extended hours on Saturdays and during peak season.
- **Planning Your Visit:** Consider weekdays for a less crowded experience, though evenings offer a special charm with illuminated shop windows.
- **Budgeting:** Be prepared for premium prices at high-end brands, but explore side streets for more affordable options.
- **Tax-Free Shopping:** If exceeding the minimum amount, inquire about tax-free shopping procedures offered by some stores.

2. Cultural and Historical Sites

2.1 Verona Cathedral (Duomo di Verona)

Verona's skyline boasts many architectural gems, and the Duomo di Verona, also known as the Cathedral of Santa Maria Matricolare, stands tall as a cornerstone of the city's religious and cultural heritage. This Romanesque masterpiece, steeped in history and artistic treasures, awaits your exploration.

History & Highlights:

- Built between the 11th and 12th centuries, the Duomo replaced two earlier churches destroyed by an earthquake. It showcases Romanesque architecture at its finest, featuring warm-colored stonework, intricate carvings, and iconic double porticos.
- Step inside and marvel at the soaring columns, arches, and frescoes depicting biblical scenes and saints.
- Explore the crypt, rumored to be the wedding venue of Shakespeare's Romeo and Juliet, adding a touch of literary intrigue to your visit.

Visiting the Duomo:

- **Location:** In the heart of the historic center, easily accessible by foot or public transportation.
- **Opening Hours:** Monday-Friday, 11 AM - 5 PM; Saturdays, 11 AM - 3:30 PM; Sundays and religious holidays, 1:30 PM - 5:30 PM.
- **Tickets:** Free entry to the church, with a small fee for the cloister and crypt. Consider the Verona Card for discounted entry and other city attractions.
- **Accessibility:** The church is partially accessible for wheelchairs, with limited access to the crypt and cloister.

Unveiling Architectural Wonders:

- **Gaze upon the facade:** Adorned with intricate sculptures and carvings depicting religious figures and mythical creatures, it sets the stage for your visit.
- **Explore the interior:** Immerse yourself in the awe-inspiring Romanesque design, featuring massive columns, towering arches, and vibrant frescoes.

- **Descend into the crypt:** Explore the atmospheric crypt, adorned with Romanesque sarcophagi and shrouded in legends about Romeo and Juliet's wedding.

Enriching Your Experience:

- **Join a guided tour:** Delve deeper into the history and artistic significance of the Duomo with a knowledgeable guide (tours available in various languages).
- **Attend a religious service:** Witness the solemnity and beauty of a Mass or vespers service, gaining a deeper understanding of the church's active role in the community.
- **Visit the adjacent Library:** Discover the Chapter Library of Verona Cathedral, one of the oldest libraries in continuous function, boasting rare manuscripts and ancient texts.

2.2 Archaeological Museum

Delve deeper into these stories at the Archaeological Museum, a treasure trove of artifacts that bring the city's Roman, Etruscan, and Medieval past to life.

History & Highlights:

- Housed in the 16th-century Palazzo Maffei, the museum showcases artifacts unearthed in and around Verona, spanning centuries of civilization.
- Explore diverse exhibits featuring Roman sculptures, intricate mosaics, everyday objects, funerary items, and weapons, offering a glimpse into daily life and artistic expression.
- Marvel at the Lapidarium, an open-air courtyard displaying impressive Roman inscriptions and architectural fragments.

Visiting the Museum:

- **Location:** Near the heart of the historic center, easily accessible by foot or public transportation.
- **Opening Hours:** Tuesday-Sunday, 8:30 AM - 6:30 PM; closed Mondays.
- **Tickets:** Entrance fee applies, with discounts available for students and groups. Consider the Verona Card for discounted entry and other city attractions.

- **Accessibility:** The museum is partially accessible for wheelchairs, with some exhibits on upper floors accessible by elevator.

Unveiling Ancient Treasures:

- **Step into Roman Verona:** Witness stunning sculptures like the Pietà di Lugnano and the portrait of Lucio Calpurnio Piso, immersing yourself in Roman artistry and culture.
- **Decipher the past with inscriptions:** Explore the Lapidarium and examine Roman funerary stelae, religious dedications, and everyday inscriptions, deciphering messages etched in stone.
- **Unearth daily life:** Discover how residents of ancient Verona lived through exhibits showcasing domestic tools, pottery, coins, and jewelry, offering a tangible connection to the past.

Enriching Your Experience:

- **Join a guided tour:** Gain deeper insights into the artifacts and their historical context with a knowledgeable guide (tours available in various languages).

- **Attend a special event or workshop:** Check for lectures, educational activities, or demonstrations related to archaeology and Roman history.
- **Combine your visit with other nearby attractions:** Explore the nearby Roman Theatre, Porta Borsari gate, or Castelvecchio Museum for a comprehensive historical experience.

Essential Tips:

- Allocate at least 1-2 hours to explore the museum comfortably.
- Download the museum app for a self-guided audio tour and additional information about specific exhibits.
- Respect the artifacts and refrain from touching or leaning on them.

2.3 Roman Theater (Teatro Romano)

Verona's vibrant cityscape holds hidden treasures, whispering tales of empires past. The Roman Theater, nestled amongst medieval and Renaissance landmarks, stands as a testament to the city's ancient legacy.

History & Highlights:

- Built in the 1st century AD, the Teatro Romano served as a vibrant entertainment venue for Roman citizens, hosting plays, musical performances, and even gladiator fights.
- Imagine the echoes of laughter and cheers resonating through the cavea (seating area) as you explore its tiered structure, still impressive today.
- Marvel at the stage (scaena) adorned with niches and statues, remnants of its once grandiose backdrop.

Visiting the Roman Theater:

- **Location:** In the heart of the historic center, easily accessible by foot or public transportation.

- **Accessibility:** The cavea offers accessible paths, while the stage area might require assistance.
- **Opening Hours:** Tuesday-Sunday, 8:30 AM - 6:30 PM; closed Mondays.
- **Tickets:** Entrance fee applies, with discounts available for students and groups. Consider the Verona Card for discounted entry and other city attractions.

Unveiling Architectural Wonders:

- **Wander through the cavea:** Imagine throngs of Romans occupying these stone seats, soaking in the performances below.
- **Stand on the stage:** Picture yourself as an actor or gladiator, feeling the historical weight of the venue beneath your feet.
- **Admire the intricate details:** Look for remnants of sculptures, decorative elements, and architectural features hinting at the theater's former grandeur.

Enriching Your Experience:

● **Join a guided tour:** Delve deeper into the history and function of the theater with a knowledgeable guide (tours available in various languages).

● **Combine your visit with the nearby Archaeological Museum:** Uncover even more artifacts and stories related to Roman Verona, creating a cohesive historical experience.

● **Attend a special event:** Check for concerts, plays, or historical reenactments held within the theater, breathing life into its ancient stones.

2 4 Lamberti Tower (Torre dei Lamberti)

Verona's skyline houses an iconic silhouette, and the Lamberti Tower stands proudly as its tallest point. This medieval marvel offers breathtaking views, historical echoes, and a unique perspective on the city.

History & Highlights:

● Built in the 12th and 15th centuries, the Lamberti Tower started as a Romanesque structure before rising higher with a Gothic extension. Its unique architectural blend reflects Verona's evolving styles.

• Witness the two bells – Marangona, signaling fires and marking hours, and Rengo, summoning citizens in times of need. Imagine their historic chimes echoing through the city.

• Marvel at the breathtaking panoramic views from the observation deck, encompassing the entire historic center, the Adige River, and surrounding hills.

Visiting the Lamberti Tower:

• **Location:** In Piazza delle Erbe, the bustling heart of the city, easily accessible by foot or public transportation.

• **Accessibility:** Stairs are the only option to reach the top, with 368 steps leading to the panoramic terrace. Consider the elevator option for a more accessible experience.

• **Opening Hours:** Daily (except December 25th), 8:30 AM - 6:30 PM.

- **Tickets:** Entrance fee applies, with discounts available for students and groups. Consider the Verona Card for discounted entry and other city attractions.

Unveiling Architectural Wonders:

- **Admire the facade:** Observe the two distinct sections, showcasing the Romanesque lower part and the Gothic upper segment, offering a visual journey through time.
- **Feel the history:** Ascend the spiral staircase, imagining medieval guards patrolling and messages relayed through bell tolls.
- **Reach the summit:** Immerse yourself in panoramic views, stretching across the cityscape, revealing hidden details and providing a fresh perspective on Verona.

Enriching Your Experience:

- **Join a guided tour:** Learn about the tower's construction, significance, and mesmerizing views with a knowledgeable guide (tours available in various languages).

- **Combine your visit with other nearby attractions:** Explore the lively Piazza delle Erbe, the Giusti Garden, or Castelvecchio Museum for a well-rounded historical experience.
- **Time your visit:** Arrive early or late to avoid peak crowds and capture the best lighting for panoramic photos.

2.5 Basilica di Santa Anastasia

Verona's historic heart overflows with captivating churches, and the Basilica di Santa Anastasia stands out as a magnificent example of Gothic architecture. This vibrant jewel, adorned with intricate sculptures and steeped in history, awaits your exploration.

History & Highlights:

- Built between the 13th and 14th centuries, the Basilica showcases impressive Gothic architecture, featuring soaring arches, ribbed vaults, and stained-glass windows depicting biblical scenes.

- Admire the magnificent pink marble facade, adorned with sculptures and intricate details depicting religious figures and stories, setting the stage for your visit.
- Step inside and marvel at the awe-inspiring interior, with its towering columns, pointed arches, and vibrant frescoes illustrating biblical narratives.
- Explore the Cappella Pellegrini, a Renaissance masterpiece adorned with frescoes by Pisanello, considered one of the finest examples of early Renaissance art in Italy.

Visiting the Basilica:

- **Location:** In the heart of the historic center, easily accessible by foot or public transportation.
- **Opening Hours:** Monday-Friday, 10 AM - 5 PM; Saturdays, 9:30 AM - 6 PM; Sundays and religious holidays, 1 PM - 5:30 PM.
- **Tickets:** Free entry to the church, with a small fee for the cloister and Pellegrini Chapel. Consider the Verona Card for discounted entry and other city attractions.

- **Accessibility:** The church is partially accessible for wheelchairs, with limited access to the cloister and Pellegrini Chapel.

Unveiling Architectural Wonders:

- **Gaze upon the facade:** Adorned with intricate sculptures and rose windows, it showcases the beauty and artistry of Gothic architecture.
- **Explore the interior:** Be captivated by the soaring columns, stained-glass windows filtering colorful light, and frescoes depicting biblical narratives.
- **Descend into the crypt:** Explore the atmospheric crypt, rumored to be the wedding venue of Shakespeare's Romeo and Juliet, adding a touch of literary intrigue.
- **Discover the Pellegrini Chapel:** Witness the vibrant frescoes by Pisanello, depicting scenes from the life of Saint George, in this Renaissance masterpiece.
- **Attend a concert:** The basilica's acoustics create a magical setting for classical music concerts, especially during the "Settembre in Musica" festival.

3. Outdoor Activities

3.1 Walks along the Adige River

Embark on a refreshing outdoor adventure by strolling along the banks of the Adige River, a vibrant artery pulsating with life and offering diverse activities for every traveler.

Scenic Walks & Bike Rides:

- **Northern Promenade:** Enjoy a leisurely walk or bike ride on the Lungadige San Giorgio, starting from Ponte Pietra. Lush greenery, stunning river views, and charming cafes line the path, offering a tranquil escape from the city buzz.
- **Southern Promenade:** Discover the Lungadige Porta Vittoria, bustling with locals and offering spectacular views of Castelvecchio and the Ponte Scaligero. Stop by the Giardino Giusti for a dose of Renaissance elegance.
- **Lover's Walk:** Rent a bike or join a guided cycling tour along the scenic path connecting Castelvecchio with

Parco dell'Adige Sud, ideal for a romantic outing or a family adventure.

Activities by the River:

- **Boat Tours:** Glide along the Adige River on a scenic boat tour, offering unique perspectives of the city's iconic landmarks and bridges. Relax and soak in the beauty while listening to historical anecdotes.
- **Birdwatching:** Channel your inner ornithologist at Parco dell'Adige Sud, a nature reserve teeming with diverse bird species. Observe heron colonies, listen to chirping warblers, and witness the graceful dance of dragonflies.
- **Fishing:** Obtain a permit and cast your line in designated areas for a relaxing afternoon. Enjoy the peaceful stillness of the river while trying your luck at catching local fish species.

Beyond the Riverbank:

- **Picnic by the River:** Pack a delicious spread and find a shady spot beneath the trees for a delightful picnic with stunning river views. Enjoy the fresh air, local delicacies, and quality time with loved ones.

- **Sunset Stroll:** As the sun dips below the horizon, paint the sky with vibrant hues, casting a magical glow on the river and bridges. Capture breathtaking photos and cherish the romantic atmosphere.
- **Open-Air Events:** Check for cultural events held along the riverbanks, like concerts, theater performances, or art exhibitions. Immerse yourself in the vibrant local scene and enjoy unique experiences under the open sky.

3.2 Cycling Tours

Embark on an unforgettable outdoor adventure by exploring the city on a cycling tour, immersing yourself in the local atmosphere and getting some exercise to boot.

Locations for Cycling Tours:

- **City Center:** Explore the historic heart of Verona with its pedestrian-only zones, piazzas, and iconic landmarks like Arena di Verona and Piazza delle Erbe. Cycle along the Adige River and discover hidden gems like Ponte Pietra and Juliet's House.

- **Parco dell'Adige Sud:** Escape the city buzz and explore the vast green expanse of Parco dell'Adige Sud. Enjoy dedicated cycling paths, observe diverse birdlife, and picnic among the trees.
- **Valpolicella:** Venture beyond the city limits and cycle through the picturesque vineyards of Valpolicella, renowned for its Amarone wine production. Enjoy breathtaking countryside views, charming villages, and authentic local experiences.
- **Lake Garda:** Combine your cycling adventure with a visit to the stunning Lake Garda. Cycle along the scenic lakeside paths, explore quaint towns like Sirmione and Bardolino, and even hop on a ferry to explore the lake from a different perspective.

Recommended Time to Go Cycling:

- **Spring (March-May):** Pleasant temperatures, fewer crowds, and blooming landscapes make for a delightful cycling experience.

- **Autumn (September-November):** Comfortable weather, vibrant autumn colors, and grape harvest season in Valpolicella add a unique touch to your tour.
- **Early Summer (June) and Late Summer (September):** Longer daylight hours offer more time for exploration, but be prepared for warmer temperatures and potential crowds.

Bike Rental Options:

- **Bike sharing:** Several companies offer bike-sharing stations throughout the city, allowing for flexible rentals at affordable prices. Look for Verona Bike Sharing or Donkey Republic.
- **Bike rental shops:** Rent various types of bikes, including hybrids, mountain bikes, and e-bikes, from numerous shops in the city center like Ways Tours, Verona Bike Tours, and Cicli Pignatti.
- **Guided tours:** Join a guided cycling tour with companies like Itinera Bike & Travel or Verona Bike Tours, and benefit from their expertise, route planning, and equipment.

Bike Rental Costs:

- **Bike sharing:** Expect around €5-10 per day or €1-2 per hour.
- **Bike rental shops:** Prices vary depending on the bike type and duration. Expect €15-30 per day for standard bikes and €30-50 for e-bikes.
- **Guided tours:** Costs typically range between €30-50 per person, depending on the tour duration, inclusions, and bike type.

3.3 Hiking in the surrounding hills

Nestled amidst its vibrant heart lie rolling green hills, beckoning outdoor enthusiasts with a tapestry of hiking trails waiting to be explored. Pack your boots and essentials, and prepare to be captivated by the beauty, tranquility, and panoramic vistas that await you.

Hiking Routes for All Levels:

- **Monte Baldo:** For seasoned hikers, conquer the majestic Monte Baldo, offering challenging ascents, diverse flora and fauna, and breathtaking views of Lake

Garda. Take the cable car from Malcesine for a head start and enjoy panoramic restaurants at the summit.

- **Lessinia Regional Park:** Immerse yourself in the vast Lessinia Regional Park, a paradise of rolling hills, charming villages, and ancient forests. Choose from various trails, like the scenic path from San Giorgio Ingannapoltron to Spiazzi di Garda, or the historical Sentiero della Grande Guerra, tracing World War I trenches.
- **Torricelle:** Discover the Torricelle Hills, a network of gentle trails perfect for families and casual hikers. Explore vineyards, olive groves, and panoramic viewpoints like the Torricella Massimiliana, offering stunning cityscapes.
- **Parco dell'Adige Sud:** Escape the city bustle and explore the Parco dell'Adige Sud, a green haven along the Adige River. Enjoy easy trails amidst lush vegetation, observe diverse birdlife, and have a picnic in the shade of towering trees.

Essential Gear for Your Hike:

- Comfortable hiking shoes or boots with good traction.
- Weather-appropriate clothing: layers for changing temperatures, sun protection, and rain gear if necessary.
- Hydration pack or water bottle: stay hydrated throughout your hike.
- Snacks and energy bars: keep your energy levels up.
- Hat and sunglasses: protect yourself from the sun.
- First-aid kit: be prepared for minor injuries.
- Map and compass or GPS: navigate the trails with confidence.
- Phone: for emergencies and to capture memories.

Benefits of Hiking in Verona's Hills:

- **Immerse yourself in nature:** escape the city noise and reconnect with the beauty of the outdoors.
- **Get some exercise:** enjoy a healthy and invigorating activity amidst stunning scenery.
- **Discover hidden gems:** explore charming villages, historical sites, and panoramic viewpoints off the beaten path.

- **Relax and unwind:** breathe in the fresh air, clear your mind, and experience tranquility in nature.
- **Capture breathtaking photos:** document your adventure with stunning landscape shots and selfies with panoramic vistas.

Additional Tips:
- Check weather conditions before heading out.
- Inform someone close to you about your planned route and estimated return time.
- Respect the environment and leave no trace.
- Be mindful of wildlife and follow local regulations.
- Combine your hike with a visit to a local winery or agriturismo for an authentic experience.

3.4 Walking Tours

Verona, the "City of Lovers," whispers it's stories not just through grand monuments, but also along its charming streets and hidden alleyways. Embark on a captivating walking tour, immersing yourself in the rich history, vibrant culture, and architectural gems that lie around every corner.

Walking Routes for Every Interest:

• **Historic Heart:** Delve into the city's past with a route encompassing iconic landmarks like the Roman Arena, Piazza delle Erbe, and Juliet's House. Learn about Roman gladiators, bustling medieval markets, and Shakespeare's timeless romance.

• **Architectural Gems:** Discover diverse architectural styles with a walk past the Scaliger Tombs, Castelvecchio, and the Gothic Basilica di Santa Anastasia. Marvel at intricate details, powerful fortresses, and artistic masterpieces.

• **Foodie Delights:** Indulge your taste buds on a culinary walking tour. Sample local cheeses, cured meats, fresh pasta, and delectable pastries at hidden trattorias and traditional markets. Uncover Verona's rich gastronomic heritage.

- **Hidden Secrets:** Escape the tourist crowds and explore off-the-beaten-path gems like the Giardino Giusti Renaissance garden, the Ponte Pietra Roman bridge, and the peaceful San Zeno Maggiore church. Discover hidden courtyards and charming alleyways.

- **Romantic Stroll:** Follow in the footsteps of Romeo and Juliet with a walk along the Adige River, Ponte dei Sospiri (Bridge of Sighs), and Juliet's balcony. Imagine their love story amidst the romantic atmosphere of the city.

4. Gardens and Parks

1. *Giardini Pubblici Arsenale (Arsenale Public Gardens)*:

- **Location:** Viale Porta Nuova, 31
- **Description:** Expansive park offering shaded avenues, a tranquil pond, a children's playground, and a small cafe for refreshments.
- **What to do:** Enjoy a relaxing stroll, go for a jog, take a boat ride on the pond, or let the kids loose in the playground.

2. *Parco di Villa Buri (Villa Buri Park)*:

- **Location:** Via Ponte San Michele, 8
- **Description:** Romantic English-style garden with winding paths, a charming lake, and various sculptures scattered throughout.
- **What to do:** Explore the diverse flora, enjoy a picnic by the lake, or attend events and exhibitions held in the park.

3. *Parco Cesare Lombroso:*

- **Location:** Lungadige S. Giorgio, 2
- **Description:** Urban park along the Adige River offering shaded walking paths, benches for relaxation, and a playground for children.
- **What to do:** Enjoy a leisurely walk with scenic river views, have a picnic under the trees, or let the kids play in the playground.

4. *Giardino Officinale Marzana (Marzana Herb Garden):*

- **Location:** Via Valdoneghe, 38
- **Description:** Educational garden showcasing a diverse collection of medicinal and aromatic plants, with workshops and events focused on herbal remedies.
- **What to do:** Learn about different herbs and their uses, participate in workshops, or simply enjoy the unique atmosphere and fragrant air.

Essential Information

- **Opening hours:** Most parks and gardens have varying opening hours, typically from morning to late afternoon. Check official websites for specific times.
- **Entrance fees:** Some gardens have entrance fees, while others are free to enter.
- **Accessibility:** Not all parks and gardens are fully accessible. Check beforehand if accessibility is a concern.
- **Activities:** Some parks offer additional activities like boat rides, playgrounds, or open-air events. Look for information online or at the entrance.
- **Combine your visit:** Pair your garden exploration with nearby attractions like museums, historical sites, or charming neighborhoods.

5. Local Cuisine and Dining

5.1 Traditional Veronese Dishes

1. Risotto all'Amarone: Indulge in the "King of Veronese Risottos." This iconic dish features Vialone Nano rice simmered in Amarone wine, a robust red known for its full-bodied flavor. Onions, butter, parmesan cheese, and sometimes beef broth complete the symphony of textures and tastes.

2. Pastissada de Caval: Take a trip back in time with this medieval masterpiece. Horse meat (traditionally, now often beef) is slow-cooked in red wine, onions, carrots, and spices, resulting in a melt-in-your-mouth, intensely flavorful stew. Served with mashed potatoes or polenta, it's a hearty and historical experience.

3. Bigoli con la Salsa al Tastasal: Twirl these delicious thick spaghetti-like noodles in a unique sauce. "Tastasal" means "taste the salt," highlighting the key ingredient - pork sausage seasoned with salt, pepper, and spices. Onions, broth, and sometimes tomato create a savory and satisfying sauce.

4. *Gnocchi di Malga:* Get a taste of mountain life with these potato dumplings. Made with ricotta cheese, flour, and eggs, these fluffy gnocchi are traditionally boiled and served with melted butter, sage, and parmesan cheese. In some variations, local mountain cheeses like Monte Veronese add a distinct bite.

5. *Tortellini di Valeggio sul Mincio:* These are not your average tortellini. Filled with a rich mixture of meat, bread, and spices, these unique "knots" hail from the town of Valeggio sul Mincio. In spring, giant versions ("Nodalini") are served during a special festival, a true spectacle for both eyes and stomach.

6. *Lessarda:* Don't miss this sweet treat. Similar to a panettone, this dome-shaped cake boasts a soft, buttery dough studded with raisins, candied fruit, and sometimes pine nuts. Its origins lie in Lessinia, a hilly region near

102

Verona, and its aroma fills the air during Christmas markets.

7. *Pandoro:* The star of the Veronese Christmas table, Pandoro is a light and airy star-shaped cake. Its airy texture comes from a long leavening process, and its flavor is simply enriched with butter, vanilla, and powdered sugar. Enjoy it plain or dusted with icing sugar for a festive touch.

♡ **Bonus Tip:** Pair your culinary adventure with local wines like Valpolicella, Bardolino, or Soave for a truly authentic Veronese experience.

5.2 Best Restaurants in Verona

1. *La Vecchia Osteria:* Michelin-starred restaurant offering an innovative take on Veronese cuisine with a focus on local, seasonal ingredients. Elegant atmosphere and impeccable service. Located Via dei Masi, 12

- **Menu:** Tasting menus change seasonally, featuring dishes like pigeon with foie gras and truffles, risotto with Vialone Nano rice and Amarone, and lamb chops with herbs. Expect modern presentations and exquisite flavor combinations.
- **Price range:** €150-200+ per person

+39 045 800 5677, (https://www.lavecchiaosteria.it/)

2. *Locanda Castelvecchio:* Romantic restaurant housed in a 14th-century building within the Castelvecchio Museum complex. Offers a refined atmosphere with frescoes and antique furniture. Located at Piazza Castelvecchio, 6

- **Menu:** Traditional Veronese cuisine with a touch of modernity. Highlights include bigoli with duck sauce, risotto with Luganega sausage, and roasted guinea fowl with polenta. Extensive wine list featuring local and Italian selections.
- **Price range:** €100-150 per person, +39 045 800 3502

3. Il Desco: Modern restaurant with a focus on contemporary Italian cuisine and creative dishes. Open kitchen concept allows guests to witness culinary artistry. Located Via Dietro Anfiteatro, 8

- **Menu:** Tasting menus with seasonal variations, featuring dishes like seared scallops with black truffle, beef cheek ravioli with Barolo sauce, and pigeon with cherries and foie gras.
- **Price range:** €120-180 per person, +39 045 800 5947.

4. Trattoria da Bacco: Cozy and traditional trattoria with a warm atmosphere and friendly service. Offers classic Veronese dishes in generous portions. Located Via Sottoriva, 13

- **Menu:** Local favorites like bigoli with various sauces, tortellini di Valeggio, and grilled meats. Vegetarian options available. Simple but delicious homemade desserts.
- **Price range:** €20-30 per person, +39 045 800 3285,

5. Osteria del Duca: Lively and historic tavern with a casual atmosphere and friendly staff. Offers typical Veronese dishes and a wide selection of local wines. Located at Vicolo San Marco, 4

- **Menu:** Traditional Veronese cuisine with daily specials. Highlights include pasta dishes like gnocchi al pomodoro and lasagna, polenta with local cheeses, and grilled sausages.
- **Price range:** €15-25 per person, +39 045 800 2594.

6. La Dispensa: Small and charming restaurant with a focus on fresh, seasonal ingredients and homemade dishes. Offers a daily changing menu and a cozy atmosphere. Located Via San Nazario, 22

- **Menu:** Varies daily based on available ingredients, typically featuring pasta dishes, soups, salads, and main courses like grilled fish or stews. Vegetarian and vegan options available.
- **Price range:** €10-20 per person, +39 045 803 0482,

These are just a few suggestions, and there are many other fantastic restaurants in Verona to suit all budgets and tastes.

5.3 Wineries of Valpolicella

Nestled amidst rolling hills, the picturesque wine region of Valpolicella beckons with its sun-drenched vineyards, centuries-old cellars, and world-renowned wines. Immerse yourself in the heart of Italian winemaking, discover the unique terroir, and embark on a captivating journey through the flavors of Valpolicella.

Winemaking in Valpolicella dates back to Roman times, and the region has earned international acclaim for its distinct styles and exceptional quality. From the iconic Amarone, a full-bodied red produced using the "appassimento" technique (drying grapes on racks), to the lighter Valpolicella and the sweet Recioto, each sip tells a story of passion, tradition, and dedication.

Valpolicella boasts diverse landscapes, encompassing gentle slopes, charming villages, and ancient stone walls. Whether you cycle through the vineyards, embark on a guided hike, or simply drive along scenic routes, the beauty of the region takes center stage. Discover hidden wineries nestled amidst the hills, each offering a unique glimpse into the local winemaking culture.

With over 400 wineries scattered across the region, choosing where to start can be overwhelming. Here are some options to help you get started:

- **For the Classic Experience:** Visit renowned wineries like Allegrini, Tedeschi, or Zenato, renowned for their iconic Amarone and Valpolicella DOC wines.
- **For Hidden Gems:** Seek out smaller, family-run wineries like Quintarelli, Giuseppe Quintarelli, or Le Salette, known for their handcrafted, limited-production wines.
- **For Unique Experiences:** Opt for wineries offering guided tours, tastings with food pairings, or special events like grape harvesting or barrel tastings.

Essential Tips for Your Wine Tour:

• **Plan your itinerary:** Decide on the areas you want to explore and research wineries that interest you. Book reservations in advance, especially during peak season.

• **Consider transportation:** Renting a car offers flexibility, but guided tours or taxis are convenient alternatives.

• **Choose your tastings:** Opt for tastings that align with your preferences and budget. Ask about different styles and grape varietals.

• **Respect the wineries:** Be mindful of opening hours and dress codes. Most wineries welcome responsible and engaged visitors.

• **Engage with the locals:** Ask questions, learn about the winemaking process, and appreciate the passion behind each bottle.

Your Valpolicella experience isn't limited to wineries. Indulge in delicious local cuisine at traditional trattorias, discover charming villages like Bardolino and San Pietro in Cariano, and explore historical sites like the Roman theater in Negrar.

5.4 Cooking Classes and Food Tours

Cooking Classes:

• **Hands-on Learning:** Get your hands dirty and learn traditional techniques. Master pasta-making, gnocchi shaping, or the art of risotto. Classes often include market visits to source fresh ingredients and end with a delicious feast of your creations.

• **Popular Options:** Opt for classic pasta and tiramisu classes, discover regional specialties like bigoli pasta or risotto all'Amarone, or explore vegetarian or gluten-free options.

• **Locations:** Several cooking schools and private homes offer classes, often centered around charming piazzas or tucked away in traditional neighborhoods.

• **Booking:** Choose individual classes or multi-day programs, and book in advance as they fill up quickly.

Prices vary depending on duration, location, and menu, typically ranging from €50-150 per person.

Food Tours:

- **Explore Hidden Gems:** Stroll through vibrant markets, taste local cheeses and cured meats, and discover hidden trattorias with knowledgeable guides. Learn about regional specialties and their history while indulging your taste buds.
- **Themed Tours:** Choose walking tours focusing on specific themes like Valpolicella wines, Veronese street food, or vegetarian delights. Explore specific neighborhoods or delve into the history of local food traditions.
- **Duration and Prices:** Tours typically last 2-4 hours, ranging from €50-100 per person, including food and drink samples. Private tours and tastings with wine pairings can be arranged for a more personalized experience.

Essentials for Your Delicious Journey:

- **Come hungry:** Prepare to savor an abundance of delicious food samples.
- **Inform allergies:** Share any dietary restrictions in advance to ensure your experience is catered to.
- **Ask questions:** Interact with your guides and locals to gain deeper insights into Veronese cuisine.
- **Visit local markets:** Immerse yourself in the sights, smells, and vibrant atmosphere of markets like Mercato Vecchio or Porta Borsari. Stock up on fresh produce, local delicacies, and souvenirs.
- **Dine at trattorias:** Seek out family-run trattorias for authentic Veronese dishes like bigoli con la salsa al tastasal or pastissada de caval.
- **Take a wine tasting:** Explore Valpolicella vineyards and indulge in tastings of Amarone, Bardolino, and other regional wines.

6. Events and Festivals

Verona's year-round calendar of events offers something for everyone. Whether you're a history buff, music lover, food enthusiast, or simply seeking a romantic escape, there's a festival or event waiting to capture your heart and create unforgettable memories. So, choose your season, plan your trip, and get ready to experience the vibrant spirit of Verona.

Spring (March-May):

- **Vinitaly (March):** Dive into the world of Italian wine at this prestigious international wine fair, showcasing hundreds of producers and tastings. (Dates vary per year)
- **Verona Marathon (April):** Challenge yourself with a half marathon or full marathon through the historic city center and scenic surrounding areas. (Dates vary per year)
- **Shakespeare in Verona (April-May):** Witness the Bard's plays come to life under the starry sky in an

open-air theatre amidst the Roman Arena. (Dates vary per year)

- **Festival della Lessinia (May):** Celebrate the traditions and flavors of the Lessinia mountain region with food stalls, music, and local crafts. (Dates vary per year)

Summer (June-August):

- **Verona Opera Festival (June-September):** Witness world-class opera performances under the magical setting of the Roman Arena, featuring renowned artists and breathtaking productions. (Dates vary per year)
- **Festa del Lacus (July):** Immerse yourself in a historical re-enactment of a Roman lake festival with boat races, costumes, and traditional Roman cuisine. (Dates vary per year)
- **Heineken Jammin' Festival (June-July):** Groove to the sounds of international and Italian music stars at this popular open-air music festival. (Dates vary per year)
- **Estate Veronese (June-August):** Enjoy a series of open-air concerts, theater performances, and cultural

events held in various piazzas and locations throughout the city. (Dates vary per year)

Autumn (September-November):

- **Tocatì:** Traditional Game Festival (September): Discover traditional games from around the world in this interactive and playful festival, perfect for families and children. (Dates vary per year)
- **Festa del Torrione (October):** Explore the historic Torrione fortress transformed into a medieval village with reenactments, crafts, and delicious food. (Dates vary per year)
- **Fiera del Tartufo (October-November):** Indulge in the king of autumn - truffles. Sample truffle-infused dishes, browse artisanal products, and learn about this precious delicacy. (Dates vary per year)
- **Verona Jazz Festival (November):** Immerse yourself in the world of jazz music with concerts, workshops, and jam sessions featuring international and local artists. (Dates vary per year)

Winter (December-February):

- **Verona Christmas Market (December):** Wander through the enchanting Christmas market in Piazza dei Signori, filled with festive stalls, twinkling lights, and traditional food and crafts. (Dates vary per year)
- **New Year's Eve Celebrations (December 31st):** Join the lively celebrations in Piazza Bra, featuring music, fireworks, and a festive atmosphere to welcome the new year.
- **Verona Carnival (February):** Immerse yourself in the colorful and vibrant carnival atmosphere with parades, masked balls, and costume contests. (Dates vary per year)
- **Valentine's Day in Verona (February 14th):** Celebrate love in the "City of Lovers" with special events, romantic dinners, and unique experiences.

7. Day Trips from Verona

7.1 Lake Garda

Lake Garda, Italy's largest lake, beckons travelers with its stunning scenery, charming towns, and diverse activities. And what better way to experience its magic than with a day trip from the enchanting city of Verona? Pack your walking shoes, swimsuit, and get ready for a day filled with beauty and adventure.

Verona and Lake Garda are well-connected, offering various options for your journey:

- **Train:** The fastest and most convenient option, with trains departing regularly from Verona Porta Nuova station and reaching Peschiera del Garda in just 13 minutes.
- **Bus:** Several bus companies operate routes between Verona and various towns around the lake, offering flexibility and affordability.

- **Car:** If you prefer the freedom of exploring at your own pace, renting a car is a great choice. The drive takes about 30 minutes, offering scenic views of the surrounding hills.

Lake Garda boasts a string of charming towns, each with its own unique character:

- **Sirmione:** Immerse yourself in medieval history at the Scaliger Castle, wander through the narrow alleys, and enjoy the thermal spa experience.
- **Bardolino:** Delight in the laid-back atmosphere, explore the vibrant harbor, and sample local wines at cozy cafes and trattorias.
- **Malcesine:** Take a cable car ride up Mount Baldo for breathtaking panoramic views, explore the Scaliger Castle, and stroll along the picturesque lakeside promenade.
- **Limone sul Garda:** Discover the charming lemon groves, indulge in local specialties like limoncello, and enjoy the tranquil atmosphere of this picturesque town.

Lake Garda caters to all interests:

• **Adventure seekers:** Hike or bike through scenic trails, try windsurfing or kitesurfing, or go rock climbing in the surrounding mountains.

• **Nature lovers:** Relax on the pebble beaches, take a boat tour to explore hidden coves and grottoes, or visit the Sigurtà Garden, a stunning oasis of flowers and nature.

• **History buffs:** Explore the Roman ruins in Sirmione, discover medieval castles and fortresses, or visit the Vittoriale degli Italiani, a stunning monument dedicated to Gabriele D'Annunzio.

• **Foodies:** Indulge in fresh lake fish and local specialties like tortellini di Valeggio and risotto al pesce persico. Don't forget to try the delicious olive oil and local wines.

Essential Tips:

• **Consider the season:** Summer offers warm weather for swimming and outdoor activities, while autumn provides vibrant foliage and fewer crowds.

- **Pack essentials:** Sunscreen, comfortable shoes, swimsuit, and a hat are crucial.
- **Purchase the Verona Card:** Offers discounted entry to attractions and free public transportation within the region.
- **Research local events:** Festivals, markets, and cultural events add another layer to your experience.
- **Pack for all weather:** The lake region experiences warm summers and mild winters. Be prepared for sunshine, rain, and potential wind.
- **Consider a boat tour:** It's a fantastic way to see the lake from a different perspective and reach hidden gems.
- **Relax and enjoy the pace:** Don't try to cram too much into your day trip. Savor the beauty, soak up the atmosphere, and embrace the laid-back Italian lifestyle.

7.2 Venice

Venice, the "City of Canals," is a must-visit for any traveler to Italy. But if you're short on time, you don't need to worry. With its proximity to Verona, a day trip from the city of Romeo and Juliet allows you to experience the magic of Venice in a whirlwind adventure.

Verona and Venice are well-connected, offering various travel options to fit your needs:

• **High-speed train:** The fastest and most comfortable option, whisking you to Venice Santa Lucia station in just under an hour. Book tickets in advance.
• **Regional train:** A more affordable option, taking approximately 1 hour and 20 minutes. Consider the longer travel time when planning your day.
• **Bus:** Several bus companies offer connections, taking around 1.5 hours. This can be a budget-friendly alternative, but factor in potential traffic delays.
• **Private tour:** Enjoy a personalized experience with a guided tour, including transportation and skip-the-line access to attractions.

Once in Venice, your exploration unfolds:

● **Embrace the canals:** Take a gondola ride, a quintessentially Venetian experience, or hop on a vaporetto (water bus) for public transportation with stunning views.

● **Wander through piazzas:** Piazza San Marco, with its iconic St. Mark's Basilica and Doge's Palace, is a must-see. Explore other charming squares like Campo Santa Margherita or Campo San Barnaba.

● **Get lost in the labyrinthine streets:** Discover hidden gems, charming bridges, and picturesque canals as you explore the city's unique layout.

● **Bridge the arts:** Visit the Gallerie dell'Accademia for Renaissance masterpieces, or admire modern art at the Peggy Guggenheim Collection.

Must-Do Experiences:

● **Climb the Campanile:** Enjoy breathtaking panoramic views of the city from St. Mark's Campanile bell tower.

- **Cross the Bridge of Sighs:** Witness the iconic bridge connecting the Doge's Palace to the prison, steeped in history and legend.
- **Indulge in Venetian delights:** Savor fresh seafood dishes, try cicchetti (small bites) with a glass of local wine, and don't miss the iconic Venetian gelato.

Planning Your Day Trip:

- **Start early:** Arrive in Venice by morning to maximize your time exploring.
- **Purchase a Venezia Unica pass:** This pass offers discounted access to public transportation and some attractions.
- **Pack smart:** Wear comfortable shoes for navigating bridges and streets, bring sunscreen and a hat, and consider a small backpack for your essentials.
- **Embrace the spontaneity:** Get lost in the city's charm, wander through hidden alleys, and discover unexpected treasures.

7.3 Milan

Craving a dose of urban chic and cultural immersion? Look no further than Milan, the fashion capital of Italy, just a short train ride away from Verona. Immerse yourself in world-class art, architectural marvels, and a vibrant atmosphere, making it the perfect day trip for history buffs, fashionistas, and curious explorers alike.

Getting from Verona to Milan is a breeze:

- **High-speed Train:** The fastest option, taking just 1 hour and 13 minutes on the Frecciarossa train. Frequent departures from Verona Porta Nuova station ensure you can maximize your time in Milan.
- **Regional Train:** A more budget-friendly option, taking about 1 hour and 50 minutes. Choose this if you prefer a slower journey and want to enjoy the scenery along the way.
- **Bus:** Though the slowest option (around 2-3 hours), it's the cheapest and offers flexibility if you're traveling on a tight budget.

Milan boasts an abundance of must-see attractions, but here are some highlights for a day trip:

- **Duomo di Milano:** Be awestruck by the intricate Gothic architecture of this iconic cathedral. Climb to the rooftop for breathtaking city views.
- **Santa Maria delle Grazie:** Witness Leonardo da Vinci's masterpiece, "The Last Supper," housed within this beautiful church and convent. Book tickets in advance to avoid disappointment.
- **Castello Sforzesco:** Immerse yourself in Milan's history at this imposing 15th-century castle, now housing museums and art collections.
- **Galleria Vittorio Emanuele II:** Shop in style at this opulent arcade, featuring luxury brands and historic cafes like the famous Camparino.
- **Teatro alla Scala:** Experience the grandeur of this world-renowned opera house, even if you don't have time for a performance. Guided tours offer a glimpse into its rich history.

If you have time, venture beyond the main attractions:

- **Navigli District:** Explore the charming canals, trendy bars, and artistic atmosphere of this revitalized area.
- **Pinacoteca di Brera:** Discover Italian art from the 14th to 20th centuries in this renowned gallery.
- **Quadrilatero d'Oro:** Indulge in a shopping spree in this "Golden Rectangle," known for its luxury fashion boutiques and designer brands.

Planning Your Day Trip:

- **Consider the season:** Spring and autumn offer pleasant weather, while summer can be hot and crowded.
- **Embrace the local cuisine:** Sample traditional Milanese dishes like risotto alla Milanese and cotoletta alla Milanese in a local trattoria.
- **Choose your focus:** Tailor your itinerary based on your interests, whether it's art, fashion, history, or simply soaking up the city's atmosphere.

- **Purchase the Milano Card:** Offers free public transportation and discounted entry to many attractions, saving time and money.
- **Embrace the "aperitivo":** Enjoy this Milanese tradition of pre-dinner drinks and snacks in a bar or cafe, experiencing the local social scene.

7.4 Vicenza

Seeking a captivating day trip from Verona, rich in history, art, and architectural wonders? Look no further than Vicenza, nestled just 28 miles away. This enchanting city boasts UNESCO World Heritage sites, Palladian architecture, and a vibrant historical center, offering a perfect escape from the bustling streets of Verona.

Reaching Vicenza is a breeze with various convenient options:

- **Train:** The fastest and most eco-friendly choice, taking just 25-58 minutes on a comfortable train ride.

Frequent departures from Verona Porta Nuova station ensure flexibility.

- **Bus:** A more budget-friendly option, taking around 45-60 minutes. Several buses connect Verona to Vicenza's central bus station.
- **Car:** Offers flexibility for exploring surrounding areas, but consider limited parking options within the historical center. The journey takes about 40 minutes via the A4 motorway.

Vicenza offers a compact and walkable historic center, allowing you to discover its gems within a day:

- **Piazza dei Signori:** Immerse yourself in the heart of the city, surrounded by iconic landmarks like the Basilica Palladiana and the Torre del Municipio (clock tower).
- **Teatro Olimpico:** Witness the architectural genius of Andrea Palladio at this UNESCO World Heritage Site, featuring the world's first permanent indoor theatre.
- **Giardino Salvi:** Relax amidst the serene beauty of this Italian-style garden, adorned with sculptures and fountains, offering a peaceful escape from the city buzz.

- **Basilica di Monte Berico:** Climb the hill for breathtaking panoramic views of Vicenza and explore the beautiful basilica with its rich history.
- **Palladian Villas:** Venture beyond the city center to discover stunning Palladian villas like Villa Capra "La Rotonda" and Villa Valmarana, showcasing the architect's signature style.

Planning Your Day Trip:

- **Consider the season:** Spring and fall offer pleasant weather for exploring, while summer can be hot and crowded.
- **Purchase the Vicenza Card:** Offers discounted entry to many attractions, free public transportation, and skip-the-line access to some sites.
- **Embrace local cuisine:** Savor authentic Vicentine dishes like "baccalà alla vicentina" (codfish) and "risotto al tastasal" (sausage risotto) in traditional trattorias.
- **Pack comfortable shoes:** The city center is best explored on foot, so be prepared for cobblestone streets and exploring different neighborhoods.

7.5 Mantua

Verona's charm is undeniable, but sometimes, a journey to a different era beckons. Enter Mantua, a UNESCO World Heritage City just 33km away, where Renaissance palaces whisper tales of grandeur and cobbled streets echo with history. Let's explore why Mantua deserves a day trip from Verona:

Reaching Mantua's Magical Embrace:

- **Train:** The fastest and most convenient option, taking just 46 minutes on a comfortable train ride. Departures from Verona Porta Nuova station are frequent.
- **Bus:** A more budget-friendly option, taking around 1 hour and 3 minutes. Buses connect Verona to Mantua Viale Mincio.
- **Car:** Offers flexibility but consider limited parking options within the city center. The journey takes about 44 minutes via the A22 motorway.

Unveiling Mantua's Treasures:

● **Palazzo Ducale:** Immerse yourself in the opulent heart of Mantua, a sprawling palace complex with stunning courtyards, frescos, and museums, once home to the Gonzaga family.

● **Piazza Sordello:** The city's vibrant main square, bustling with cafes and shops, offering a glimpse into daily life and a chance to people-watch.

● **Palazzo Te:** Escape to the countryside and explore this architectural gem, designed by Giulio Romano, featuring stunning gardens and frescos with mythological scenes.

● **Basilica di Sant'Andrea:** Witness the artistic genius of Leon Battista Alberti in this Renaissance masterpiece, known for its dome and harmonious proportions.

● **Casa del Mantegna:** Visit the former home of Renaissance painter Andrea Mantegna, now a museum showcasing his works and offering insights into his life.

Planning Your Day Trip:

• **Consider the season:** Spring and fall offer pleasant weather for exploring, while summer can be hot and crowded.

• **Purchase the Mantua Card:** Offers discounted entry to many attractions and free public transportation, saving time and money.

• **Embrace "La Cucina Mantovana":** Savor local specialties like "tortelli di zucca" (pumpkin ravioli) and "risotto alla pilota" (rice with sausage) in traditional trattorias.

8. Nightlife and Entertainment

Verona isn't just about Romeo and Juliet's romantic whispers; it also boasts a vibrant nightlife scene catering to diverse tastes. Whether you seek lively bars, stylish clubs, or intimate jazz lounges, Verona has something for everyone.

Bars & Pubs:

- **Piazza Erbe:** This bustling square transforms into a lively hub at night, with cafes and bars spilling onto the piazza. Enjoy a spritz at Caffe Mazzanti or a craft beer at La Birreria Mazzanti.

- **Borgo San Zeno:** This historic neighborhood offers a charming atmosphere with local pubs and wine bars. Sample local wines at Enoteca Il Cavatappi or enjoy live music at Osteria del Duca.

- **Corso Porta Nuova:** This trendy area is lined with modern bars and pubs, perfect for people-watching and socializing. Check out The King's Head for British pub vibes or Bar Luce for creative cocktails.

Clubs & Discos:

• **Stadio area:** This area near the Verona Arena offers several larger nightclubs, playing electronic and dance music. Check out The Club for mainstream hits or Echoes for a more underground vibe.

• **Centro Storico:** While smaller, the historical center also boasts a few nightclubs. Alchimia is a popular choice for techno and house music, while Rumors Club offers a diverse range of genres.

• **Summer Events:** During summer, outdoor venues like Arena di Verona and Giardino Shakespeare host special events like concerts and DJ sets, offering a unique nightlife experience.

Tips for a memorable night out:

● **Dress code:** While most places are relaxed, some clubs might have a dress code, so check beforehand.

● **Public transportation:** Verona has a good public transportation system that runs late at night, making it easy to get around.

● **Safety:** Verona is generally a safe city, but be aware of your surroundings and avoid isolated areas late at night.

● **Local customs:** Italians typically start their evenings later, with dinner around 9 pm and nightlife peaking after 11 pm.

9. Markets and Shopping Souvenirs

Verona is also a paradise for shoppers with diverse options ranging from bustling local markets to elegant designer boutiques. Prepare to indulge your shopping desires with this guide to Verona's market and shopping scene:

Local Delights:

• **Mercato Vecchio (Old Market):** Immerse yourself in the lively atmosphere of this daily market, open from 7:30 am to 1:30 pm. Browse stalls overflowing with fresh produce, local cheeses, cured meats, artisan crafts, and souvenirs.

• **Porta Borsari Market:** Held every Sunday morning from 8 am to 1 pm, this market offers a wider range of goods, including antiques, clothing, and household items alongside fresh produce and local specialties.

- **Giardino Giusti Farmers Market:** Every Wednesday morning from 9 am to 1 pm, local farmers showcase their fresh seasonal produce and artisanal products in the beautiful setting of Giusti Gardens.

Souvenir Treasures:

- **Locally-made crafts:** Look for hand-painted ceramics, glassware, and leather goods, often featuring iconic Verona landmarks or Romeo and Juliet themes.
- **Food and drink specialties:** Bring home a taste of Verona with local wines like Bardolino or Amarone, regional cheeses like Grana Padano, and cured meats like Soppressa Veneta.
- **Verona-themed souvenirs:** Find fridge magnets, keychains, and t-shirts adorned with Verona's iconic sights or Romeo and Juliet motifs.

Fashion Finds:

- **Via Mazzini:** This elegant pedestrian street is Verona's main shopping artery, lined with luxury brands like Gucci, Prada, and Armani.

- **Corso Porta Borsari:** Discover a mix of high-end and mid-range fashion brands, including Italian favorites like Max Mara and Pinko.
- **Corso Sant'Anastasia:** This charming street offers a mix of independent boutiques, local designers, and artisan workshops for unique finds.

Shopping Tips:

- **Opening hours:** Most shops are open from 9 am to 7 pm, with shorter hours on Sundays and Mondays. Markets typically operate in the mornings.
- **Sales:** Look for summer sales in July and August, and winter sales in January and February.
- **Bargaining:** While not expected in most stores, it's common at flea markets and antique shops.
- **Tax-free shopping:** If you're a non-EU resident and spend over €154 in a single store, you can claim a VAT refund.
- **Cash vs. cards:** Most stores accept credit cards, but having some cash on hand is always helpful for smaller purchases or markets.

Apart From the Stores:

● **Department stores:** La Rinascente in Piazza delle Erbe offers a wide range of designer brands and luxury goods.

● **Outlet centers:** If you're looking for deals, head to the Scaligera Village outlet center near Verona for discounted designer brands.

● **Antique shops:** Explore the narrow streets around Piazza delle Erbe for hidden gems and unique vintage finds.

10. Verona for Families

Verona is a vibrant city with plenty to offer families of all ages. From enchanting piazzas to exciting adventures, get ready to create lasting memories with your little ones:

History with a Twist:

- **Climb the Lamberti Tower:** Enjoy breathtaking city views while kids spot the whale bone hanging from the top.
- **Explore Castelvecchio Museum:** Discover suits of armor, weapons, and fascinating exhibits that bring history to life.
- **Join a gladiator school workshop:** Dress up like a gladiator and learn sword-fighting techniques at the Arena di Verona.

Outdoor Adventures:

- **Rent bikes and cycle along the Adige River:** Enjoy scenic trails and fresh air, with plenty of gelato stops along the way.
- **Splash around at Canevaworld water park:** Cool off on thrilling slides, wave pools, and a pirate-themed adventure area.
- **Take a boat tour on Lake Garda:** Witness stunning landscapes and charming towns from a different perspective.

Creative Fun:

- **Make pizzas at a cooking class:** Learn the art of pizza making and enjoy your delicious creations afterwards.
- **Watch a puppet show in Piazza delle Erbe:** Be entertained by traditional puppeteers and their colorful marionettes.
- **Participate in a family art workshop:** Get creative and paint your own masterpieces in a fun and interactive setting.

Sweet Treats and Family Moments:

• **Indulge in authentic gelato:** Sample different flavors and enjoy the vibrant atmosphere of local gelaterias.

• **Picnic in Giardino Giusti:** Relax amidst beautiful gardens, fountains, and grottos, perfect for a family picnic.

• **Have a movie night under the stars:** Enjoy open-air cinema screenings at various locations throughout the summer.

Additional Tips:

• **Purchase the Verona Card:** Offers discounted entry to attractions, free public transportation, and skip-the-line access, saving time and money.

• **Take breaks and prioritize fun:** Plan in rest periods and activities that cater to everyone's interests.

• **Embrace the Italian family-friendly atmosphere:** Enjoy leisurely meals, relaxed schedules, and the welcoming nature of locals.

11. Verona on a Budget

Verona, the city of romance and Romeo & Juliet, doesn't have to empty your wallet. Explore its historical charm, artistic wonders, and vibrant atmosphere with these budget-friendly activities:

Free & Fascinating:

- **Piazza delle Erbe:** Immerse yourself in the lively heart of Verona, bustling with market stalls, cafes, and street performers. Enjoy the free entertainment and soak up the atmosphere.
- **Arena di Verona:** Marvel at this iconic Roman amphitheater from outside. Entrance is free, and you can often catch glimpses of rehearsals or events happening inside.
- **Ponte Pietra:** Stroll across this historic Roman bridge, offering stunning views of the Adige River and Castelvecchio.

- **Duomo di Verona:** Explore the beautiful cathedral, free to enter and showcasing impressive artwork and architecture.
- **Basilica di San Zeno Maggiore:** Witness the impressive Romanesque architecture and intricate details of this church, featuring a free crypt with fascinating frescoes.
- **Window-shopping:** Explore the elegant streets of Via Mazzini and Corso Porta Borsari, admiring designer boutiques and charming local shops.

Exploring Beyond the Free:

- **Verona Card:** Consider purchasing the Verona Card for discounted entry to several attractions, free public transportation, and skip-the-line access, saving you money in the long run.
- **Walking tours:** Join free walking tours offered by local guides, gaining insights into the city's history and hidden gems.

- **Public transportation:** Utilize the efficient bus system to reach different areas of the city at an affordable cost.
- **Picnics in the park:** Pack a delicious picnic and enjoy lunch amidst the greenery of Giardino Giusti or Parco delle mura.
- **Local cuisine:** Skip expensive restaurants and indulge in delicious and affordable local dishes like "bigoli" (thick pasta) with ragu or "tortellini di zucca" (pumpkin ravioli) at traditional trattorias.

Hidden Gems:

- **Giardino Giusti:** Discover this hidden treasure, a Renaissance garden adorned with grottos, fountains, and beautiful landscaping. Enjoy the peaceful atmosphere for just €7 entry fee.
- **Teatro Romano:** Explore the ruins of this ancient Roman theater, offering a glimpse into Verona's past for a €2.50 ticket.
- **Castel San Pietro:** Hike up the hill for panoramic views of the city and explore the charming castle ruins, free to enter.

12. Romantic Things To Do In Verona

Verona pulsates with an undeniable romantic charm. Beyond Shakespeare's iconic love story, Verona offers countless experiences to ignite passion and create lasting memories with your sweetheart.

Stroll Hand-in-Hand:

- **Ponte Pietra:** Stroll hand-in-hand across this ancient Roman bridge, whispering sweet nothings as you admire the sunset painting the Adige River gold.
- **Giardino Giusti:** Get lost in the romantic labyrinthine paths of this Renaissance garden, adorned with hidden grottos, trickling fountains, and blooming flowers. Share a stolen kiss beneath the shade of a cypress tree.
- **Romeo's Courtyard:** Visit the supposed balcony where Juliet declared her love, now adorned with love letters and padlocks symbolizing eternal love.

Candlelit Evenings:

- **Opera Under the Stars:** Witness a breathtaking operatic performance at the Arena di Verona under the starlit sky, the music weaving a spellbinding atmosphere.
- **Dinner Cruise on Lake Garda:** Embark on a romantic cruise on the picturesque Lake Garda, enjoying a delicious candlelit dinner and breathtaking views as the sun dips below the horizon.
- **Wine Tasting in Bardolino:** Savor local wines with your loved one in a charming vineyard amidst rolling hills, sharing laughter and creating memories over every sip.

Whispers of History:

- **Secret Juliet's House Tour:** Take a special tour of Juliet's House after hours, avoiding the crowds and immersing yourselves in the romantic ambience as you whisper secrets beneath the balcony.
- **Castel San Pietro:** Hike up the hill for breathtaking panoramic views of the city, sharing a romantic picnic as the golden light bathes Verona in magic.

- **Secret Courtyard of Palazzo Miniscalchi:** Discover this hidden gem, a peaceful courtyard adorned with frescoes and sculptures, offering a haven of tranquility for whispered promises and stolen kisses.

Extra Touches of Romance:

- **Ride in a Horse-Drawn Carriage:** Glide through the cobbled streets in a horse-drawn carriage, recreating a fairytale moment with your loved one.
- **Gondola Ride in Venice:** Take a day trip to Venice and serenade your partner with a romantic gondola ride through the canals, whispering sweet nothings under the Rialto Bridge.
- **Cooking Class for Two:** Learn the art of making pasta or pizza together, a fun and interactive experience that ends with a delicious meal you can share.

Travel Journal

PART THREE: ESSENTIAL PRACTICAL TRAVEL INFORMATION

Now that you've been swept away by the charm and possibilities of your chosen destination, it's time to get down to the nitty-gritty of planning your trip. This section equips you with the essential practical information needed for a smooth and stress-free journey. We'll cover everything from transportation options and accommodation tips to local customs and money saving advice. Sit tight as we dive into the practicalities that will make your trip a dream come true.

1. Visa and Entry Requirements

Verona welcomes visitors from across the globe, but understanding visa and entry requirements is crucial for a smooth and stress-free journey. This guide provides a comprehensive overview of visa regulations specific to different regions, ensuring your trip to Verona starts on the right note.

Entering as a European Citizen:

- **EU Citizens:** If you're a citizen of the European Union (EU), Switzerland, Iceland, Liechtenstein, Norway, or San Marino, you don't need a visa to enter Italy for stays up to 90 days within any 180-day period. Simply carry a valid passport or national ID card for identification purposes.

- **Non-EU Citizens with EU Residence Permit:** If you hold a valid residence permit issued by an EU country, you can also enter Italy visa-free for stays up to 90 days within the validity of your permit.

Traveling from the USA, UK, Canada, and Australia:

- **Visa-Free Entry:** Travelers from the United States, United Kingdom, Canada, and Australia are fortunate to enjoy visa-free entry to Italy for stays up to 90 days within any 180-day period. However, ensure your passport is valid for at least three months beyond your intended departure date from Italy.

Coming from Asia and Africa:

- **Visa Requirements Vary:** Visa requirements for citizens from Asian and African countries vary depending on your nationality. Here's a general overview:
- **Visa-Free:** Citizens from Japan, South Korea, Israel, and Singapore are typically visa-exempt for stays up to 90 days.
- **Schengen Visa:** Citizens from many other Asian and African countries require a Schengen visa to enter Italy. This visa allows travel within the Schengen area, which includes Italy and 25 other European countries.

Types of Schengen Visa:

- **Short-Stay Visa (C Visa):** Issued for stays up to 90 days within any 180-day period, ideal for tourism, business meetings, or visiting family and friends.

- **Long-Stay Visa (D Visa):** Issued for stays exceeding 90 days, typically required for studies, work, or residency purposes.

Crossing the Border:

- **Passport Control:** Upon arrival in Italy, you'll need to pass passport control. Present your passport and any required visa (if applicable) to the immigration officer.
- **Supporting Documents:** Depending on your visa type and nationality, you may be asked for additional documents, such as proof of onward travel, accommodation bookings, or financial means.

Additional Resources:

- **Italian Ministry of Foreign Affairs:** (https://travel.state.gov/content/travel/en/international-travel/International-Travel-Country-Information-Pages/Italy.html)
- **Schengen Visa Information:** (https://www.schengenvisainfo.com/)

♡ **Stay Informed:** Visa regulations can change, so it's crucial to check the latest information with the relevant authorities or Italian embassy/consulate in your home country before your trip.

- This information is intended as a general guide and may not apply to all individual circumstances.
- Always consult the official sources mentioned above for the most up-to-date and accurate visa requirements.

2. Getting to Verona

Flying into Verona Airport (VRN):

Verona Villafranca Airport (VRN) is the main gateway to the city, conveniently located just 12 kilometers away. Numerous airlines connect Verona to major cities worldwide, offering options for every budget and preference.

From Europe and Germany:

• **Direct flights:** Airlines like Lufthansa, Alitalia, KLM, and British Airways offer direct connections from major European cities like Frankfurt, Munich, Amsterdam, and London. Journey times range from 1-2 hours.

• **Connecting flights:** Many other European cities offer convenient connections via major hubs like Milan Malpensa or Rome Fiumicino.

From the USA and Canada:

- **Direct flights:** Delta Air Lines offers seasonal direct flights from New York JFK to Verona, with a flight time of approximately 8.5 hours.
- **Connecting flights:** Most major US and Canadian cities offer connections via European hubs like Frankfurt, Munich, or Paris. Expect journey times ranging from 12-18 hours.

From the UK:

- **Direct flights:** Airlines like Ryanair and easyJet offer direct flights from London Stansted and Manchester to Verona, with flight times around 2-2.5 hours.
- **Connecting flights:** Other UK airports offer connections via European hubs.

From Asia and Africa:

- **Connecting flights:** Due to distance, direct flights from Asia and Africa are rare. Expect connections via major European hubs like Frankfurt, Paris, or

Amsterdam. Journey times can vary significantly depending on your origin and chosen route.

Airport Arrival and Transfers:

• **Immigration:** Upon arrival, proceed to passport control and present your travel documents. If required, have your visa and supporting documents readily available.

• **Baggage Claim:** Collect your luggage from the designated carousel for your arriving flight.

• **Transportation:** Several options connect you from the airport to Verona city center:

• **Taxis:** Taxis are readily available outside the arrivals hall. Fares are fixed and displayed, with a typical cost of around €30-€40 to the city center. Contact details for authorized taxi companies are available at the airport information desk.

• **Aerobus shuttle:** The Aerobus shuttle departs every 20 minutes, connecting the airport to Verona Porta Nuova train station with a one-way fare of €8.

- **Public bus:** Public buses offer a budget-friendly option, departing every 30 minutes. Tickets can be purchased at machines inside the arrivals hall or onboard for €6.
- **Pre-booked private transfers:** For convenience and a personalized experience, consider pre-booking a private transfer directly to your hotel or accommodation.

Additional Tips:

- **Download essential apps:** Consider downloading apps for offline maps, language translation, and public transportation information for added convenience.
- **Be aware of jet lag:** Adjust your sleep schedule gradually before your trip, especially if traveling from long distances.
- **Learn basic Italian phrases:** A few basic greetings and essential phrases can go a long way in navigating the city and interacting with locals.

Additional Resources:

- Verona Airport website: (https://www.aeroportoverona.it/en/)
- Aerobus shuttle: (https://www.atv.verona.it/Autobus_per_aeroporto_Catullo)
- Italian Ministry of Foreign Affairs: (https://travel.state.gov/content/travel/en/international-travel/International-Travel-Country-Information-Pages/Italy.html)

3. Booking Cheap Flights

Explore the world for less, travel to stunning destinations from anywhere for prices as low as $400. I've snagged flights from the UK, USA, and Asia for under $50 by following these smart strategies:

1. Incognito Mode FTW: Use private browsing (incognito mode) when searching for flights. Airlines sometimes offer lower prices to first-time visitors, so masquerading as a new user can unlock hidden deals.

2. Hunt for Errors & Deals: Be a deal detective! Websites and airlines occasionally list erroneous fares due to technical glitches or currency conversions. Check resources like Scott's Cheap Flights, Airfare Watchdog, or Jack's Flight Clubs for error fares and special offers.

3. Flight Aggregators are Your Allies: Tools like Google Flights and Skyscanner are your booking powerhouses. They compare prices across airlines and show you daily price fluctuations. Skyscanner's "Explore" feature even lets you discover budget-friendly destinations based on your budget.

4. *Comparison is Key*: Don't settle for the first option! Compare prices across platforms like Kayak and Hopper and set price alerts to snag deals the moment they drop.

5. *Fly Free with Points*: Loyalty programs are your ticket to free flights! Sign up for travel rewards credit cards or airline frequent flyer programs to earn points on every purchase. These points can be redeemed for free flights and accommodation, making your travel dreams a reality.

Bonus Tips for Budget Travel

- **Embrace Flexibility:** Be open to adjusting your travel dates by a few days or weeks. This can significantly impact prices, especially during peak seasons.

- **Skip the Direct:** Consider connecting flights instead of direct routes. While it might take longer, the savings can be substantial.
- **Early Bird Gets the Deal:** Booking flights in advance often offers better fares. Start your search a few months ahead for optimal deals.
- **Airline Loyalty:** While comparing is crucial, focusing on one airline can unlock perks and potential upgrades over time.
- **Clear Your Cookies:** Deleting browsing cookies can occasionally reset prices and reveal hidden offers.

With a little planning and these travel hacks, you can unlock incredible experiences at a fraction of the cost. Get out there and explore the world for less.

4. Getting Around Verona

Verona offers a convenient and efficient transportation system to help you explore every corner. Lets equip you with the essential information to navigate Verona like a local, maximizing your time and enjoyment.

Public Transportation:

- **Buses:** Verona's bus network (ATV) covers the city extensively, operating from 6:00 am to 00:30 am. Single tickets cost €1.30, with day passes and multi-day passes available for more economical travel. You can purchase tickets at tobacco shops, newsstands, or onboard the bus using machines (exact change required). Download the ATV (Azienda Trasporti Verona) mobile app for real-time bus information and route planning.

Useful routes:

Line 11: Connects the city center with Castelvecchio and Porta Nuova train station.

Line 21/22: Connects the city center with Juliet's House and Castel San Pietro.

Line 70: Connects Verona with Lake Garda for day trips.

- **Funicolare:** This funicular railway connects the city center with Castel San Pietro, offering stunning views and convenient access to the castle. Round-trip tickets cost €5.

- **Taxis:** Taxis are readily available at designated taxi ranks throughout the city, including the train station and Piazza Bra. Fares are metered and start at approximately €4, with additional charges for luggage and nighttime rides. Contact details for authorized taxi companies are often displayed at taxi ranks or available at tourist information points.

- **Bicycle Rentals:** Verona Bike, the city's bike-sharing program, offers affordable rentals (€2 for 30 minutes, €5 for a day) at various stations across the city. Ideal for exploring at your own pace and enjoying the fresh air.
- Website: (https://bikeverona.it/en/)

Several private companies also offer bike rentals, often providing guided tours or themed cycling experiences.

• **Walking:** The historic city center is compact and pedestrian-friendly, making walking a delightful way to discover hidden gems and soak in the atmosphere. Be aware of designated pedestrian zones where vehicles are restricted.

Additional Information:

• **Verona Card:** Consider purchasing the Verona Card for discounted entry to major attractions, free public transportation within the city limits, and skip-the-line access at select venues.

• **Luggage storage:** If you arrive early or have late departure, luggage storage facilities are available at the train station and some hotels.

• **Accessibility:** Most public transportation options are wheelchair-accessible, and many tourist attractions cater to individuals with disabilities.

Local Taxi Operators:

- Radiotaxi Verona: +39 045 532 666
- Consorzio Taxi Verona: +39 045 858 1403
- Radiotaxi Essedue: +39 045 820 6000

Don't Forget to;

- Validate your bus ticket upon boarding, even if purchased beforehand.
- Purchase taxi rides only from authorized companies at designated ranks.
- Be mindful of pedestrian zones and traffic regulations when cycling.

5. Top Rental Companies

If you want to venture beyond the city center and explore the rolling hills of the surrounding countryside, the charming towns around Lake Garda, or the picturesque villages nestled amidst vineyards. Renting a car provides the freedom and flexibility to explore at your own pace and discover hidden gems off the beaten path. Here's a breakdown of the top rental companies in Verona to help you choose the perfect fit for your needs:

1. Maggiore Rent:

- **Contact:** Via Centro, 35, 37019 Verona, Italy | +39 045 820 0434 | (https://www.maggiore.it/en/)

- **Packages:** Offers a variety of packages, including basic, comfort, and premium, with varying insurance coverage and mileage options. Prices start around €30 per day for a small car.

- **Requirements:** Valid driver's license, credit card, and passport. Additional fees may apply for young drivers or one-way rentals.

- **Pros:** Extensive fleet of vehicles, convenient locations, online booking with real-time availability, good customer service reviews.

- **Cons:** May not offer the most competitive prices, additional insurance options can add up.

2. Hertz:

- **Contact:** Verona Airport (VRN), Via Strada della Diga, 37069 Villafranca, Italy | +39 045 800 9242 | (https://www.hertz.com/rentacar/reservation/)

- **Packages:** Offers various packages with different levels of insurance and roadside assistance. Prices start around €35 per day for a small car.

- **Requirements:** Valid driver's license, credit card, and passport. Additional fees may apply for young drivers or one-way rentals.

- **Pros:** Well-known brand, reliable service, convenient airport location, online booking with various options.

- **Cons:** Prices can be higher than some local companies, limited flexibility in mileage options.

3. Sixt:

- **Contact:** Verona Porta Nuova Railway Station, Piazzale 25 Aprile, 37122 Verona, Italy | +39 045 800 1360 | (https://www.sixt.com/car-rental/)

- **Packages:** Offers various packages with different levels of coverage and additional services. Prices start around €25 per day for a small car.

- **Requirements:** Valid driver's license, credit card, and passport. Additional fees may apply for young drivers or one-way rentals.

- **Pros:** Competitive prices, wide range of vehicles, good online booking experience, loyalty program benefits.

- **Cons:** May have limited availability during peak season, customer service reviews can be mixed.

4. Locauto Rent:

- **Contact:** Verona Airport (VRN), Viale Alfredo Noack, 37069 Villafranca, Italy | +39 045 850 0284 | (https://www.locautorent.com/en/)

- **Packages:** Offers basic, comfort, and full insurance packages. Prices start around €20 per day for a small car.

- **Requirements:** Valid driver's license, credit card, and passport. Additional fees may apply for young drivers or one-way rentals.
- **Pros:** Affordable prices, transparent fees, good customer service reviews, loyalty program discounts.
- **Cons:** May have a smaller fleet selection compared to larger companies, limited locations.

5. Europcar:

- **Contact:** Verona Porta Nuova Railway Station, Piazzale 25 Aprile, 37122 Verona, Italy | +39 045 800 9863 | (https://www.europcar.com/en-us)
- **Packages:** Offers various packages with different levels of insurance and roadside assistance. Prices start around €30 per day for a small car.
- **Requirements:** Valid driver's license, credit card, and passport. Additional fees may apply for young drivers or one-way rentals.
- **Pros:** Well-known brand, reliable service, convenient locations, loyalty program benefits.
- **Cons:** Prices can be higher than some local companies, customer service reviews can be mixed.

Choosing the right rental company in Verona

● **Type of vehicle:** Select a car that suits your needs (size, automatic/manual, features) and driving style.

● **Coverage:** Understand the insurance options and choose the level of coverage that fits your comfort level and budget.

● **Mileage:** Consider your planned itinerary and choose a package with appropriate mileage allowance or unlimited options.

● **Additional fees:** Be aware of any additional fees for young drivers, one-way rentals, fuel charges, or airport taxes.

● **Reviews:** Read online reviews from other travelers to get insights into customer service, vehicle condition, and overall experience.

● **Location:** Choose a company with convenient pick-up and drop-off locations, especially if you're arriving or departing by train or airport.

● **Book in advance:** Booking your car rental in advance can guarantee availability and potentially secure better deals.

- Check fuel policy: Understand the fuel policy (full-to-full, pre-paid fuel) and fill up accordingly to avoid extra charges.
- **Inspect the vehicle:** Carefully inspect the car for any damage before driving off and document any existing issues.
- **Be familiar with traffic rules:** Learn about Italian traffic regulations and driving etiquette to ensure a safe and enjoyable journey.

6. Best Areas to Stay, Accommodation

Verona offers diverse neighborhoods, each with its own charm and appeal. Choosing the right one can elevate your experience. Here's a guide to the best areas, considering distance from the airport and unique reasons to stay:

For history buffs and first-time visitors:

• **Historic Center (Città Antica):** Immerse yourself in the heart of Verona, steps from iconic sights like the Arena and Juliet's House. Bustling piazzas, charming cafes, and romantic atmosphere abound. Distance from airport: 12 km (~25 min by taxi or shuttle).

Accommodation
- **Hotel Scaligeri:** Immerse yourself in history and elegance at this 5-star hotel housed in a 14th-century palace. Enjoy frescoed ceilings, a rooftop terrace with panoramic views, and a Michelin-starred restaurant.

Amenities include a spa, fitness center, and concierge service. Price range: €500-€1000 per night. Contact: +39 045 800 1500, https://www.booking.com/hotel/it/hotelcasascaligeri.html

- **Locanda al Vescovo:** This charming B&B offers comfortable rooms with traditional Italian decor and a warm atmosphere. Enjoy a delicious breakfast served in the courtyard garden. Amenities include free Wi-Fi and luggage storage. Price range: €80-€150 per night. Contact: +39 045 800 4134, https://www.locandavescovo.it/en/

For budget-conscious travelers:

• *Veronetta:* Escape the tourist crowds and explore this vibrant, authentic neighborhood on the east side of the Adige River. Affordable accommodations, local trattorias, and a laid-back vibe await. Distance from airport: 14 km (~30 min by taxi or shuttle).

Accommodation

- Palazzo Victoria: This boutique hotel housed in a 16th-century palace offers a blend of modern luxury and historical charm. Enjoy spacious rooms with antique furniture, a rooftop terrace with city views, and a Michelin-starred restaurant. Amenities include a spa, fitness center, and concierge service. Price range: €400-€800 per night. Contact: +39 045 595 600, https://www.fivestaralliance.com/luxury-hotels/verona/palazzo-victoria

- Airis Verona: This modern hostel offers clean and comfortable dorm rooms and private rooms, perfect for budget-conscious travelers. Enjoy a shared kitchen, common areas for socializing, and free Wi-Fi. Price range: €30-€60 per night. Contact: +39 045 800 1144, https://www.tripadvisor.ie/ShowUserReviews-g187871-d6945125-r306596925-B_B_Agli_Scavi-Verona_Province_of_Verona_Veneto.html

For families and nature lovers:

- ***Borgo Trento:*** Enjoy a peaceful, residential area north of the center, surrounded by green spaces and parks like Giardino Giusti. Family-friendly restaurants, quiet streets, and easy access to Lake Garda. Distance from airport: 10 km (~20 min by taxi or shuttle).

Accommodation

- **Villa Mosconi:** This 5-star villa offers a luxurious retreat with stunning views of the surrounding hills and vineyards. Enjoy elegant rooms with private balconies, an outdoor pool, a Michelin-starred restaurant, and a spa. Amenities include a fitness center, tennis courts, and concierge service. Price range: €600-€1200 per night. Contact: +39 045 595 566, https://villamosconi.com/italian-menu-new-york/

- **B&B al Ponte:** This family-run B&B offers cozy rooms with a garden view and a friendly atmosphere. Enjoy a delicious homemade breakfast served in the common room. Amenities include free Wi-Fi and bicycle rentals. Price range: €50-€100 per night. Contact: +39 347 022 1316, https://www.foreververona.it/en/

For a unique local experience:

• **San Zeno:** Discover Verona's historic charm beyond the main tourist areas. Explore the beautiful Basilica di San Zeno and lively Piazza San Zeno, known for its local markets and trattorias. Distance from airport: 13 km (~30 min by taxi or shuttle).

Accommodation

- **Hotel Due Torri:** This 5-star hotel boasts a prestigious location near the Basilica di San Zeno and offers stunning views of the city. Enjoy elegantly furnished rooms, a rooftop terrace with a pool, and a Michelin-starred restaurant. Amenities include a spa, fitness center, and concierge service. Price range: €700-€1500 per night. Contact: +39 045 595 044, https://hotelduetorri.duetorrihotels.com/en/luxury-hotel-5-stars-verona/hotel

- **Locanda Maragona:** This charming B&B offers a comfortable stay in a historic building near the Basilica di San Zeno. Enjoy spacious rooms with antique furniture, a shared garden, and a delicious breakfast. Amenities include free Wi-Fi and luggage storage. Price range: €60-€120 per night. Contact: +39 045 800 0307, https://www.tripadvisor.com/Restaurant_Review-g18787 1-d16658974-Reviews-La_Locanda-Verona_Province_o f_Verona_Veneto.html

For luxury and exclusivity:

- ***Parco delle Mura:*** Indulge in a refined atmosphere near the ancient city walls. Luxurious hotels, upscale restaurants, and stunning views of the city and countryside create an unforgettable stay. Distance from airport: 15 km (~35 min by taxi or shuttle).

Accommodation
- **Villafranca Resort & Spa:** Nestled within the Parco delle Mura, this 5-star resort offers a tranquil escape with breathtaking views of the city and surrounding hills.

Enjoy spacious suites with private balconies, an outdoor pool, a Michelin-starred restaurant, and a world-class spa. Amenities include a fitness center, tennis courts, and concierge service. Price range: €800-€2000 per night. Contact: +39 045 860 0630

- **Ai 2 Mori:** This historic guesthouse within the city walls offers charming rooms with antique furniture and a peaceful atmosphere. Enjoy a delicious homemade breakfast served in the garden courtyard. Amenities include free Wi-Fi and access to a shared kitchen. Price range: €40-€80 per night. Contact: +39 348 356 8270

Tips for Booking Your Dream Accommodation in Verona

Verona's diverse neighborhoods offer accommodation options for every budget and style. Here are some expert recommendations to help you find the nice and perfect place to stay:

Consider Your Preferences:

• **Budget:** Set a realistic budget and compare prices across different booking platforms and hotel websites.

• **Travel Style:** Choose a neighborhood that matches your pace, whether you prefer the historical heart or a quieter area.

• **Amenities:** Prioritize features like breakfast, spa access, or a balcony based on your needs.

• **Travel Dates:** Book well in advance, especially during peak season (spring and summer).

Booking Strategies:

• **Comparison Websites:** Use Kayak, Skyscanner, or Trivago to compare prices and deals across multiple platforms.

• **Hotel Websites:** Check official hotel websites for special offers or packages.

• **Local B&Bs and Hostels:** Consider charming B&Bs or hostels for a more authentic experience and potentially lower prices.

- **Read Reviews:** Look for recent reviews on platforms like TripAdvisor to get insights from other travelers.
- **Contact the Hotel Directly:** Contact the hotel for personalized assistance or to negotiate rates, especially for longer stays.

Additional Tips:

- Look for deals like early bird discounts, packages with sightseeing tours, or loyalty program benefits.
- Consider staying outside the city center for lower prices and easier parking, with good public transportation access.
- Be flexible with your dates if possible, as prices can vary significantly depending on the day of the week.
- Don't hesitate to ask questions and clarify any concerns with the hotel before booking.
- Read the cancellation policy carefully before booking.

7. Comprehensive Packing Checklist

Clothing:

- Comfortable walking shoes for exploring the historic city
- Lightweight and breathable clothing for the summer months
- Layers for cooler evenings, especially in spring and autumn
- Jacket or coat for colder seasons
- Swimwear if you plan to visit Lake Garda or nearby lakes
- Hat and sunglasses for sun protection
- Umbrella or rain jacket for unexpected showers

Travel Essentials:

- Passport, visa, and any required travel documents
- Travel insurance information
- Flight and accommodation details
- Local currency and credit cards
- Power adapter and chargers for electronic devices

- Portable power bank for on-the-go charging
- Travel-sized toiletries and personal hygiene items

Health and Safety:
- Prescription medications and a copy of the prescription
- Basic first aid kit with pain relievers, bandages, and any necessary medications
- Health insurance card and emergency contact information
- Sunscreen with a high SPF
- Insect repellent
- Face masks and hand sanitizer for public spaces

Electronics:
- Camera or smartphone for capturing memories
- Travel-friendly camera accessories (tripod, extra memory cards)
- E-reader or tablet for entertainment
- Headphones for a comfortable journey and private listening
- Travel-sized portable speakers for impromptu picnics

Outdoor and Activities:

- Comfortable daypack for excursions
- Water bottle to stay hydrated
- Snacks for energy during walks and tours
- Comfortable backpack or bag for daily use
- Guidebook or travel app for navigating the city
- Binoculars for enjoying scenic views

Cultural and Dressing Up:

- Smart-casual clothing for dining out or attending performances
- Modest clothing for visiting religious sites
- Comfortable yet slightly formal attire for special events or festivals
- Lightweight scarf or shawl for covering shoulders in churches or cool evenings

Entertainment and Leisure:

- Reading material or e-books for downtime
- Travel-sized games or cards for leisure
- Sketchbook or journal for recording your experiences

- Multi-language phrasebook for basic communication

Extras:

- Reusable shopping bag for local market finds
- Padlocks for attaching love locks, if you plan to visit Juliet's House
- Foldable travel umbrella for unexpected rain
- Travel sewing kit for quick fixes
- Collapsible daypack for additional storage during day trips

By carefully packing these essentials, you'll be well-prepared for a seamless and enjoyable holiday in Verona. Tailor this checklist to your specific needs and the time of year you plan to visit for an even more personalized packing experience.

8. Staying Safe and Healthy

Accommodation Safety:

- **Choose reputable accommodations:** Opt for licensed and well-reviewed hotels, hostels, or B&Bs. Check online reviews and safety features like secure locks and fire alarms.

- **Secure your belongings:** Use hotel safes for valuables and keep room doors and windows locked when you're out. Be mindful of pickpockets, especially in crowded areas.

- **Be aware of fire exits:** Familiarize yourself with emergency exits and evacuation procedures upon check-in.

Moving Around:

- **Walking:** Explore the city center on foot during the day, but be cautious in poorly lit areas at night.

- **Public transport:** Utilize buses, trams, and taxis for longer distances. Validate tickets and be aware of potential pickpockets.

- **Taxis:** Use licensed taxis from designated ranks or pre-book reputable companies. Agree on fares upfront and avoid sharing cabs with strangers.
- **Driving:** If renting a car, be familiar with Italian traffic rules and drive defensively. Use designated parking areas and avoid leaving valuables in the vehicle.

Public Transport Safety:

- **Validate tickets:** Always validate your tickets on buses and trams to avoid fines.
- **Beware of pickpockets:** Keep valuables secure, especially in crowded areas. Avoid carrying large sums of cash.
- **Be respectful:** Be aware of local customs and avoid eating or drinking on public transport.
- **Ask for help:** If you feel unsafe or need assistance, don't hesitate to ask bus drivers, station personnel, or local authorities.

Food Safety:

- **Stick to reputable restaurants:** Choose establishments with good hygiene practices and fresh ingredients. Avoid street food if unsure of its origin.
- **Drink bottled water:** Tap water is generally safe, but opt for bottled water to be cautious, especially outside the city center.
- **Be mindful of allergies:** Inform restaurants of any food allergies you have and choose dishes accordingly.
- **Wash your hands:** Wash your hands regularly, especially before eating, to avoid stomach upsets.

Activity Safety:

- **Choose reputable tour operators:** Opt for licensed and insured companies for guided tours, especially for adventurous activities like hiking or bike tours.
- **Follow instructions:** Listen carefully to safety instructions and adhere to guidelines, especially at historical sites or during water activities.

• **Wear appropriate clothing and footwear:** Dress comfortably and according to the chosen activity to avoid injuries.

• **Sun protection:** Apply sunscreen regularly, especially during the summer months, and wear sunglasses and hats.

Emergency Contact Numbers:

• **Emergency Services:** Dial 112 for police, ambulance, and fire services.

• **Tourist Police:** +39 045 800 4984 for assistance with tourist-related issues.

• **Hospital:** Azienda Ospedaliera Universitaria Integrata Verona: +39 045 812 1111

9. Finance and Money Saving Tips

Flights:

- **Flexibility is key:** Be flexible with travel dates and consider flying on weekdays or during shoulder seasons (spring and fall) for cheaper fares.
- **Compare airlines and booking platforms:** Utilize aggregators like Skyscanner or Kayak to compare prices across airlines and booking platforms.
- **Consider budget airlines:** While offering fewer amenities, budget airlines like Ryanair or easyJet can offer significantly lower fares, especially for short-haul flights.
- **Sign up for airline newsletters:** Get notified about flash sales and special offers directly from your preferred airlines.

Accommodation:

- **Explore alternative options:** Consider cozy B&Bs, family-run guesthouses, or hostels for a more affordable and authentic experience compared to large hotels.

- **Stay outside the city center:** Look for accommodations in nearby towns or neighborhoods with good public transportation links, often at lower prices.
- **Utilize travel rewards programs:** Redeem accumulated points or miles for hotel stays, potentially saving a significant amount.
- **Book in advance:** Secure your accommodation early, especially during peak season, to take advantage of early bird discounts.

Transportation:

- **Embrace public transportation:** Verona's efficient bus system offers affordable passes for unlimited travel within specific timeframes.
- **Walk whenever possible:** Explore the charming city center on foot to save on transportation costs and soak in the atmosphere.
- **Consider cycling:** Rent a bicycle for a budget-friendly and healthy way to explore the city and surrounding areas.

- **Share taxis:** If opting for taxis, split the fare with fellow travelers to reduce individual costs.

Food:

- **Skip tourist traps:** Avoid overpriced restaurants catering specifically to tourists and seek out authentic local trattorias or family-run eateries.
- **Embrace street food:** Sample delicious and affordable paninis, arancini, and other local delights from street vendors.
- **Picnics in the park:** Grab groceries from local markets and enjoy a budget-friendly picnic in one of Verona's beautiful parks.
- **Self-catering options:** Choose accommodations with kitchen facilities to prepare your own meals, potentially saving significantly on dining out.

Activities:

- **Seek free options:** Explore Verona's numerous free attractions like historical landmarks, public squares, and churches.

- **Consider Verona Card:** If planning several paid attractions, invest in the Verona Card for discounted entry and free public transportation.
- **Look for discounts and special offers:** Many museums and attractions offer discounted rates on specific days or times, such as student or senior discounts.
- **Join free walking tours:** Discover hidden gems and learn about local history with free walking tours offered by passionate guides.

Additional Tips:

- **Pack light:** Avoid baggage fees by packing efficiently and utilizing checked baggage strategically.
- **Utilize free Wi-Fi:** Many hotels, cafes, and public spaces offer free Wi-Fi, allowing you to stay connected without racking up data charges.
- **Shop at local markets:** Immerse yourself in the local culture and find unique souvenirs at affordable prices at farmers' markets or street markets.

10. Useful Apps and Websites

General Planning and Travel:

- TripAdvisor: (https://www.tripadvisor.com/) - Reviews and recommendations for hotels, restaurants, attractions, and activities.
- Rome2rio: (https://www.rome2rio.com/) - Multimodal travel search engine to compare routes, prices, and durations for flights, trains, buses, and ferries.
- TheFork: Online reservation platform for restaurants, offering deals and discounts.
- GetYourGuide: (https://www.getyourguide.com/) - Platform for booking tours, activities, and skip-the-line tickets.
- Google Maps: (https://www.google.com/maps) - Navigation app with public transportation information, walking directions, and live traffic updates.

Accommodation:

● **Booking.com:** (https://www.booking.com/) - Popular booking platform for hotels, apartments, and other accommodations.

● **Hostelworld:** (https://www.hostelworld.com/) - Booking platform for hostels and budget-friendly accommodations.

● **Airbnb:** (https://www.airbnb.com/) - Platform for booking unique homestays and apartments.

Transportation:

● Trenitalia: (https://www.trenitalia.com/en.html) - National train operator, offering ticket booking and journey planning.

● Thello: Low-cost train operator connecting Verona with other Italian cities.

Activities and Tours:

● Opera Arena di Verona: (https://www.arena.it/en/) - Official website of the Arena di Verona, offering information on opera performances and ticket booking.

Bonus Apps:

- Duolingo: (https://www.duolingo.com/) - Learn basic Italian phrases for easier communication.
- XE Currency Converter: (https://www.xe.com/currencyconverter/) - Convert currencies on the go.
- WiFi Map: (https://wifimap.io/) - Find free Wi-Fi hotspots around the city.

Remember to download any offline maps or essential apps before your trip to avoid data roaming charges. With these resources and a bit of planning, you're all set for a smooth and enjoyable vacation in Verona.

11. A Guide to Sports Activities in Verona

Verona is also a haven for sports enthusiasts, whether you're a seasoned athlete or a casual player, the city offers diverse options to get your adrenaline pumping and enjoy the sunshine.

Outdoor Activities:

- **Cycling:** Rent a bike and explore the city's network of bike paths, including the scenic Adige River trail. You can choose the option of joining a guided tour or venture out independently.
- **Hiking:** Lace up your boots and conquer the Lessinia Mountains, offering breathtaking views and challenging trails. Check difficulty levels and choose wisely.
- **Running:** The city center is ideal for jogging, with flat routes around the Arena and Giardino Giusti park. Look out for pedestrian zones and traffic.
- **Swimming:** Take a refreshing dip in public pools like Piscine Le Grazie or Piscine Santini. Alternatively, enjoy

Lake Garda's beaches for swimming, windsurfing, and paddleboarding.

- **Tennis:** Numerous public and private courts are available for booking, including those near Parco delle Mura offering stunning city views.
- **Rock climbing:** Challenge yourself at the AGES climbing gym, perfect for all skill levels.

Organized Activities:

- **Football (Soccer):** Watch a match at the historic Stadio Bentegodi, home to Serie A team Hellas Verona. Catch pre-game festivities and soak in the passionate atmosphere.
- **Horseback riding:** Explore the countryside on horseback with various ranches offering guided tours and lessons for all levels.
- **Golf:** Tee off at the Golf Club Paradiso del Garda, a scenic 18-hole course nestled between the city and the lake. Book tee times in advance.

- **Water sports:** Lake Garda is a haven for water enthusiasts. Try windsurfing, kitesurfing, or stand-up paddleboarding with certified instructors at local centers.

- **Gear rentals:** Many shops offer bike, helmet, and other equipment rentals for your convenience.
- **Weather:** Dress appropriately for the season and sun protection is essential, especially during summer.
- **Public transport:** Buses and trains connect you to various outdoor locations, making exploration easy.
- **Opening hours:** Check opening times and schedules for public pools, courts, and sports facilities before heading out.
- **Local rules:** Be mindful of local regulations and restrictions regarding specific activities, especially in protected areas.

12. Job Opportunities in Verona

Verona, with its rich cultural heritage and economic vibrancy, offers diverse job opportunities across various sectors. Whether you are a local resident or an expatriate, navigating the job market in Verona requires a blend of cultural understanding and professional skills.

1. *Tourism and Hospitality:*

- **Roles:** Hotel management, tour guides, hospitality professionals, event coordinators.
- **Opportunities:** Verona's status as a major tourist destination creates a demand for skilled professionals in the tourism and hospitality sector.

2. *Education:*

- **Roles:** Teaching positions in language schools, international schools, and universities.
- **Opportunities:** Verona's reputation as a cultural hub attracts students and educators, providing opportunities for those in the education field.

3. Manufacturing and Industry:

- **Roles:** Engineers, technicians, production managers.

- **Opportunities:** Verona's industrial sector, including manufacturing and machinery, contributes significantly to the local economy.

4. Information Technology (IT):

- **Roles:** Software developers, IT consultants, system administrators.

- **Opportunities:** As technology continues to advance, there is a growing demand for IT professionals to support various industries.

5. Fashion and Design:

- **Roles:** Fashion designers, graphic designers, retail management.

- **Opportunities:** Verona has a strong connection to fashion and design, offering opportunities in the retail and creative sectors.

6. *Agriculture and Viticulture*:

- **Roles:** Viticulturists, agricultural specialists, farm managers.

- **Opportunities:** The surrounding region is known for its vineyards and agriculture, creating jobs in the agribusiness sector.

7. *Health and Wellness*:

- **Roles:** Healthcare professionals, wellness coaches, fitness instructors.

- **Opportunities:** Verona has a well-established healthcare system, and the wellness industry is gaining traction.

8. *International Organizations*:

- **Roles:** Project managers, policy analysts, language specialists.

- **Opportunities:** Verona's strategic location and international appeal attract professionals working with global organizations and institutions.

9. Business and Finance:

- **Roles:** Accountants, financial analysts, business consultants.

- **Opportunities:** Verona's thriving business environment offers various roles in finance, accounting, and consulting.

10. Language Services:

- **Roles:** Translators, interpreters, language instructors.

- **Opportunities:** With a diverse international presence, there is a demand for language-related services in Verona.

11. Arts and Culture:

- **Roles:** Curators, artists, cultural event coordinators.

- **Opportunities:** Verona's rich cultural heritage creates openings in arts management and event planning.

Job Search Resources:

- Explore local job portals, such as Verona Jobs and Veneto Lavoro.
- Networking through industry events and online platforms is crucial.
- Consider contacting recruitment agencies with a presence in Verona.

Cultural Considerations:

- Understanding Italian culture and language can enhance your job prospects.
- Building a professional network and establishing personal connections are integral in Verona's business environment.

As you navigate the job market in Verona, tailor your approach based on your skills, industry trends, and cultural awareness. The city's unique blend of tradition and modernity offers a dynamic backdrop for individuals seeking diverse and fulfilling career opportunities.

13. Tour Operator Companies

1. Verona In Tour:

- Website: (https://veronaintour.com/)
- Phone number: +39 045 800 1535

Types of Tours:

• **Bike tours:** Explore the city and its surroundings on a leisurely bike ride. Choose from various themed tours, including historical tours, food tours, and wine tours.

• **Walking tours:** Discover Verona's hidden gems and must-see sights on a guided walking tour. Options include romantic tours, historical tours, and food tours.

• **Day trips:** Venture beyond Verona and explore nearby destinations like Lake Garda, Sirmione, and Mantova. Choose from wine tasting tours, historical tours, and scenic boat tours.

• **Cooking classes:** Learn how to prepare traditional Veronese dishes in a fun and interactive cooking class. They offer different classes for all skill levels.

2. *Ways Tours:*

- Website: (https://waystours.com/destination/visit-verona/)

- Phone number: +39 045 570 1561

Types of Tours:

• **Walking tours:** Immerse yourself in Verona's history and culture on a guided walking tour. Options include skip-the-line tours of the Arena di Verona, Juliet's House, and Castelvecchio.

• **Food tours:** Discover Verona's culinary scene on a delicious food tour. Sample local specialties like pasta, cheese, and wine at hidden trattorias and artisan shops.

• **Day trips:** Explore nearby towns and villages like Lake Garda, Sirmione, and Valpolicella. Choose from wine tasting tours, historical tours, and scenic boat tours.

• **Bike tours:** Cycle through the city's charming streets and admire the beautiful views. Options include guided tours and self-guided rentals.

3. Verona Tours:

- Website: (https://www.veronatours.com/)
- Phone number: +39 348 903 4238

Types of Tours:

● **Walking tours:** Discover Verona's history and culture on a guided walking tour. Options include themed tours like "Romeo and Juliet," "Verona by Night," and "Legends and Ghosts."

● **Food tours:** Indulge in Verona's delicious food scene on a guided food tour. Sample local specialties like pasta, pizza, and gelato at hidden trattorias and artisan shops.

● **Wine tours:** Explore the Valpolicella wine region and visit renowned wineries. Learn about the winemaking process and enjoy tastings of local wines.

● **Opera tickets:** Book your tickets to see a world-class opera performance at the Arena di Verona. Choose from various productions throughout the summer season.

4. Top Travel Team:

- Website: (https://toptravelteam.it/)
- Phone number: +39 045 800 5167

Types of Tours:

- **Walking tours:** Explore Verona's historical center and hidden gems on a guided walking tour. Options include skip-the-line tours of the Arena di Verona and Juliet's House.

- **Bike tours:** Enjoy a leisurely bike ride through the city and its surroundings. Choose from various themed tours, including historical tours, food tours, and wine tours.

- **Day trips:** Venture beyond Verona and explore nearby destinations like Lake Garda, Sirmione, and Mantova. Choose from wine tasting tours, historical tours, and scenic boat tours.

- **Cooking classes:** Learn how to prepare traditional Veronese dishes in a fun and interactive cooking class. They offer different classes for all skill levels.

14. Etiquette and Customs

1. *Greetings and Politeness*:

- **Greetings:** Italians generally greet with a warm handshake and may exchange kisses on the cheek, especially among friends.

- **Politeness:** Use "buongiorno" (good morning), "buonasera" (good evening), and "buonanotte" (good night) based on the time of day.

2. *Dress Code*:

- **Modesty:** When visiting churches or more formal settings, dress modestly. Avoid beachwear in city centers.

- **Smart-Casual:** Many restaurants appreciate smart-casual attire, especially in the evening.

3. *Dining Etiquette*:

- **Reservations:** It's advisable to make reservations, especially in popular restaurants.

- **Tipping:** Service charges are often included, but leaving small change is appreciated. Tipping is not as necessary as it is in some other countries.

4. *Language*:

- **Italian Phrases:** While many locals speak English, learning a few basic Italian phrases can enhance your experience and show respect.
- **Volume:** Italians value a conversational tone; speaking loudly in public places may be considered impolite.

5. *Public Behavior*:

- Queueing: Form orderly queues in public spaces and transportation.
- Piazza Delle Erbe: While Piazza delle Erbe is bustling, refrain from feeding pigeons to maintain cleanliness.

6. *Cultural Sites*:

- **Quiet Respect:** When visiting churches and historical sites, maintain a quiet and respectful demeanor.

- Photography: Respect posted signs regarding photography restrictions in certain areas.

7. *Greetings at Juliet's House*:

- Courtyard Etiquette: In Juliet's House courtyard, be mindful of other visitors. Touching Juliet's statue for good luck is a tradition.

8. *Transportation*:

- **Valid Tickets:** Ensure you have a valid ticket for public transportation, and validate it when required.

- **Pedestrian Zones:** Be cautious in pedestrian zones and watch for bicycles.

9. *Waste Management*:

- **Littering:** Dispose of waste responsibly. Keep in mind that littering is discouraged and can result in fines.

10. *Shopping*:

- **Shopping Hours:** Many shops close for a few hours in the afternoon, especially smaller establishments.

- **Bargaining:** Bargaining is not a common practice in regular shops but may be acceptable in markets.

11. *Cultural Sensitivity:*

- **Religious Sites:** Dress modestly when entering religious sites, covering shoulders and knees.
- **Respect Customs:** Respect local customs and traditions, especially during religious or cultural events.

By embracing these etiquette tips, you'll not only navigate Verona with ease but also contribute to the positive interaction between tourists and the local community.

15. Suggested Itineraries

5 Days Solo Adventure Itinerary

Day 1: Historic City Stroll

- **Morning:** Explore Piazza Bra, marvel at the Arena di Verona.

- **Afternoon:** Wander through Piazza delle Erbe, visit Juliet's House.

- **Evening:** Savor Italian cuisine in a local trattoria.

Day 2: Hilltop Views and Castles

- **Morning:** Hike to Castel San Pietro for panoramic city views.

- **Afternoon:** Visit Castelvecchio, admire its medieval architecture.

- **Evening:** Relax along the Adige River promenade.

Day 3: Wine Tasting in Valpolicella

- **Morning:** Head to Valpolicella wine region.

- **Afternoon:** Tour vineyards and enjoy wine tastings.
- **Evening:** Return to Verona for a delightful dinner.

Day 4: Lakeside Excursion to Lake Garda

- **Morning:** Day trip to Lake Garda by train or bus.
- **Afternoon:** Explore Sirmione or Garda town.
- **Evening:** Lakeside dinner with stunning views.

Day 5: Cultural Discoveries and Farewell

- **Morning:** Visit Basilica di San Zeno Maggiore.
- **Afternoon:** Explore Verona's hidden gems and local markets.
- **Evening:** Final stroll through the historic center, savoring gelato.

5 Days Family Fun Vacation Itinerary

Day 1: Fairytale Beginnings

- **Morning:** Explore Juliet's House and courtyard.
- **Afternoon:** Enjoy a family-friendly lunch in Piazza delle Erbe.

- **Evening:** Attend a kid-friendly performance at the Arena di Verona.

Day 2: Castle Quest

- **Morning:** Visit Castelvecchio and its family-friendly museum.

- **Afternoon:** Stroll along the riverbanks or take a boat ride.

- **Evening:** Dinner at a local pizzeria.

Day 3: Enchanting Gardens and Parks

- **Morning:** Spend time at Giardino Giusti's beautiful gardens.

- **Afternoon:** Picnic in Parco delle Mura or Parco Sigurtà.

- **Evening:** Gelato treat in Piazza Bra.

Day 4: Lake Adventure to Gardaland

- **Full Day:** Excursion to Gardaland, Italy's largest theme park.

- **Evening:** Relax and dine at the lakeside.

Day 5: Culture and Creativity

- **Morning:** Visit Museo di Castelvecchio for family-oriented exhibits.

- **Afternoon:** Explore the Children's Museum (Museo Africano).

- **Evening:** Farewell dinner at a family-friendly osteria.

Tips:

- Check for family discounts at attractions.
- Keep hydrated; carry water and snacks.
- Use comfortable strollers for younger kids.
- Plan breaks for rest and play.
- Embrace the family-friendly ambiance of Verona.

5 Days of Romantic Bliss

Day 1: Romantic Beginnings

- **Morning:** Stroll through Piazza delle Erbe for a charming start.

- **Afternoon:** Visit Juliet's House and courtyard for a touch of romance.

- **Evening:** Candlelit dinner in a romantic restaurant.

Day 2: *Wine and Love in Valpolicella*

- **Morning:** Head to Valpolicella for a wine tour.

- **Afternoon:** Wine tasting in vineyards with picturesque views.

- **Evening:** Romantic dinner in a winery.

Day 3: *Lakeside Retreat to Lake Garda*

- **Morning:** Day trip to Lake Garda, explore charming lakeside towns.

- **Afternoon:** Relax by the lake and enjoy a boat ride.

- **Evening:** Lakeside dinner with a view.

Day 4: *Sunset at Castel San Pietro*

- **Morning:** Visit Castelvecchio for a cultural experience.

- **Afternoon:** Hike to Castel San Pietro for sunset views.

- **Evening:** Intimate dinner in the city center.

Day 5: Culinary Delights and Farewell

- **Morning:** Explore local markets for gourmet delights.

- **Afternoon:** Cooking class together or a food tour.

- **Evening:** Romantic farewell dinner in a fine dining restaurant.

16. Basic Italian Phrasebook

Greetings and Politeness:

1. Hello - Ciao

2. Good morning - Buongiorno

3. Good evening - Buonasera

4. Good night - Buonanotte

5. How are you? - Come stai? (informal) / Come sta? (formal)

Common Expressions:

6. Please - Per favore

7. Thank you - Grazie

8. You're welcome - Prego

9. Excuse me / I'm sorry - Scusa (informal) / Mi scusi (formal)

10. Yes - Sì / No - No

Getting Around:

11. Where is...? - Dov'è...?

12. How much is this? - Quanto costa?

13. Can you help me? - Puoi aiutarmi? (informal) / Può aiutarmi? (formal)

14. I don't understand - Non capisco

15. Where is the bathroom? - Dov'è il bagno?

Numbers:

16. 1 - Uno / 2 - Due / 3 - Tre / 4 - Quattro / 5 - Cinque

17. 10 - Dieci / 20 - Venti / 50 - Cinquanta / 100 - Cento

18. How much does it cost? - Quanto costa?

Eating Out:

19. I would like... - Vorrei...

20. The check, please - Il conto, per favore

21. Water - Acqua / Wine - Vino

22. Delicious - Delizioso

23. I'm a vegetarian - Sono vegetariano/a

24. Can I have the menu? - Posso avere il menù?

Emergency Phrases:

25. Help! - Aiuto!

26. I need a doctor - Ho bisogno di un medico

27. Where is the nearest hospital? - Dove si trova l'ospedale più vicino?

28. I've lost my... - Ho perso il/la mio/mia...

29. Call the police - Chiama la polizia

Shopping:

30. How much does it cost? - Quanto costa?

31. I would like to buy... - Vorrei comprare...

32. Do you accept credit cards? - Accettate carte di credito?

Cultural Courtesies:

33. May I take a photo? - Posso fare una foto?

34. What time is it? - Che ora è?

35. Have a nice day! - Buona giornata!

Remember to speak with a smile and embrace the local culture. Learning a few basic Italian phrases will not only enhance your travel experience but also show your appreciation for the Italian way of life.

CONCLUSION

As you bid farewell to Verona, you're not just leaving a city; you're departing from a canvas of emotions painted with the hues of history, the melodies of romance, and the warmth of genuine Italian hospitality. Verona, with its cobblestone streets and ancient walls, has woven its tales into the fabric of your journey.

From the timeless romance of Juliet's balcony to the grandeur of the Arena, Verona beckons visitors to become a part of its narrative, to dance with its traditions, and to savor the richness of its culture. Each winding alleyway, each whispered sonnet, echoes the heartbeat of a city that has stood the test of time and embraced the modern world without losing its soul.

As you carry the memories of Verona with you, may the echoes of the operatic arias from the Arena linger in your heart. May the taste of Amarone wine transport you back to the sun-kissed vineyards of Valpolicella. And may the spirit of Verona, where Shakespearean tales come to life and where love stories are written in the starlit evenings, stay eternally alive in your wanderlust soul.

Verona, with its enchanting fusion of past and present, is more than a destination; it's a sanctuary for dreamers, a symphony for lovers, and a gallery of memories waiting to be painted. As you step away, remember the laughter shared in Piazza delle Erbe, the whispers exchanged under Juliet's balcony, and the timeless beauty that unfolded with every sunset over the Adige.

Until we meet again, may the charm of Verona accompany you on your onward journey, and may the enchantment of this city forever reside in the tapestry of your travels.

Arrivederci, dear traveler, until the day Verona calls you back to its embrace. Verona will forever be the sweetest parting, a city that captured not just your itinerary but your heart.

Travel Journal

Travel Journal

Travel Journal

Travel Journal

Travel Journal

1. Top Attractions in Verona

```
S O M N Z Y V Y D Q G J I Q Q D Z T G P
J X E O E Z C C H Y W T H Z M O E M O R
O M I L N Y U T E I L U J I N A J I T T
N I C T T E A W N J T A T N O V C J N L
X Q X B R S Z J I H X U D E S A J Q F F
G B D K L E A   T Z H B S I S K O Y S A
R O H X Q J B C N L G U K T A Z Z A I P
L G L I W D E M S A M N E U N M R Y B R
X J V S Y T I E A T S L M E B T O W U S
U A C I L I S A B L V T Z F I Q K Y E C
R A E F O Z A R T E I P   E T N O P P A
F G T Z P O L R C X G P K Y C Z G Z Y L
S R Y Z A W I C G O Z X I O H A I T E I
O M O U D R H Z R E M O T V R N A V W G
F G I H H I E T A B B A R D Z Z R B S E
B G M W O B A N P R B J E X M A D S Z R
E Y T H K E Y J A M C N B G L D I B N K
P S O H T F Z X O M S O M O R X N M I K
Z M Q J V N H T D I N T A Q B P O U G X
E Z O R E G I L A C S L L L X U P G B U
```

- Arena
- Juliet
- Castle
- Ponte Pietra
- Piazza
- Giardino
- Lamberti
- Basilica
- Museo
- Castelvecchio
- Gardens
- Tomba
- Lamberti
- Scaliger
- Romeo
- Arco
- Duomo
- Scaligero
- Teatro
- San Zeno

229

2. Must Try Local Dishes

P	Q	W	A	E	N	V	E	O	R	T	H	M	V	F	E	H	A	A	M
A	U	K	I	T	L	L	T	Z	I	J	U	T	N	M	Y	X	D	T	M
M	E	A	O	V	N	A	W	N	S	G	S	I	S	A	P	T	A	A	M
A	X	A	S	I	G	E	P	C	I	O	I	A	H	T	F	P	S	R	O
R	D	G	V	E	C	Z	L	Z	F	W	M	M	I	S	O	X	S	R	R
O	R	O	F	G	R	C	Z	O	R	Y	A	A	Z	U	U	U	I	U	O
N	P	Z	N	O	Y	B	I	Q	P	E	R	R	L	Y	R	E	T	B	D
E	H	P	X	N	O	I	A	T	O	G	I	E	C	V	R	X	S	E	N
O	F	M	M	A	Y	G	D	W	S	S	T	T	I	T	L	V	A	J	A
R	W	L	A	D	O	O	S	X	A	A	T	T	W	S	K	Z	P	J	P
C	Z	D	S	A	W	L	Y	R	C	W	P	I	K	K	H	M	E	A	F
I	B	J	L	P	W	I	D	T	N	X	E	C	F	N	D	T	D	G	H
W	G	V	N	C	W	E	D	T	P	B	X	M	S	M	G	L	E	E	O
K	N	N	P	S	N	H	N	F	A	W	E	V	B	M	I	V	J	N	T
D	O	L	O	Y	C	I	E	C	I	S	O	P	P	R	E	S	S	A	T
N	J	A	A	C	R	S	C	Y	R	R	I	S	O	T	T	O	D	G	P
D	L	U	O	I	C	A	H	G	S	I	S	D	O	Q	J	T	C	U	W
S	P	I	E	L	L	H	J	U	T	D	F	V	M	C	C	V	F	L	F
F	R	A	B	À	H	J	I	A	D	R	V	Q	W	Q	P	Z	T	R	H
O	V	G	B	V	L	S	C	T	O	R	T	E	L	L	I	N	I	Z	U

- Amarone
- Risotto
- Polenta
- Baccalà
- Bigoli
- Pastissada
- Gnocchi
- Soppressa
- Tortellini
- Fegato
- Sarde
- Rabà
- Risi
- Luganega
- Pasticcio
- Burrata
- Tiramisu
- Pandoro
- Amaretti
- Padano

230

3. Top Tourist Cities in Italy

```
F C R B H V J P A M R A P O M R E L A P
M E T K Y A N O R E V J S B W C C W Y O
R M L L O A T B Y R K P R Q V U N A Q A
M C M O R J G T A X B O L O G N A G U A
T R N A L I M D I Q K E Q W H E J D W L
G C A A J S B G N C O C F L T M A F L Y
T B S I E N A F A H H V U S X P Y E T M
A F Q G E Q L T T H Q R E G M R C Z O R
R E L U R O L R A E F I G G W C V Z B A
Q I D R R H X R C V R E Q Y E T U R I N
Y I Y E V V Y M C T N B T S E M O R P E
P L N P H H V W A O J H V E T F P A X I
K C C W W B G N A I N V J L G U U T G M
E W B X W Z C U V G Q C P P S F P U B D
S Y W O M A G R E B T D J A X Y U I Z N
T P N B M T T Z A M K A C N A U Q K S S
U Q O F R B U K T T A N N E V A R R Z A
X F C H B R C B C Z M E C I N E V V A R
H X U S I T N F Z J Z O Y L G C A Z H B
O F Y U Y D N J Q V D T E A U W P A K Y
```

- Rome
- Milan
- Florence
- Venice
- Naples
- Turin
- Bologna
- Genoa
- Palermo
- Verona
- Pisa
- Siena
- Perugia
- Bergamo
- Catania
- Padua
- Parma
- Lecce
- Ravenna
- Trieste

Puzzle 1 solution

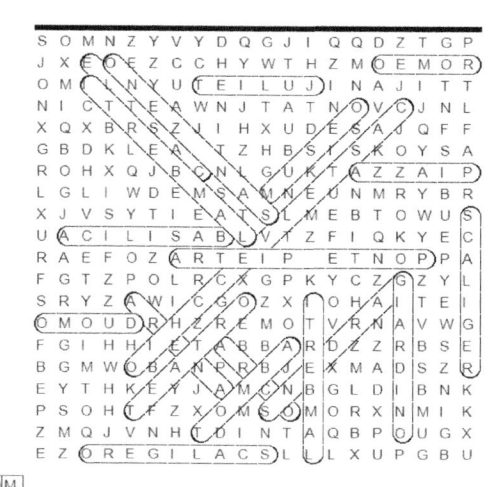

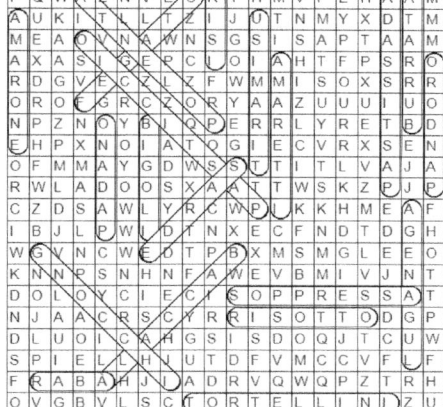

Puzzle 2 solution

Puzzle 3 solution

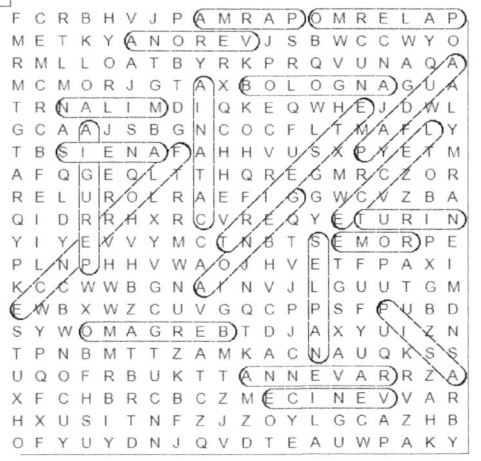

232

VERONA ITINERARY PLANNER

Day 1: Activities

Day 2: Activities

Day 3: Activities

Day 4: Activities

VERONA ITINERARY PLANNER

Day 5: Activities

Day 6: Activities

Day 7: Activities

Day 8: Activities

VERONA ITINERARY PLANNER

Day 9: Activities

Day 10: Activities

Day 11: Activities

Day 12: Activities

VERONA ITINERARY PLANNER

Top Attractions To See

Local Dishes To Try

Total Budget

Total Expenses

Printed in Great Britain
by Amazon